A. M Rowan

History of Ireland

As Disclosed by Irish Statutes Passed by Irish Parliaments Between 1310 and 1800

A. M Rowan

History of Ireland
As Disclosed by Irish Statutes Passed by Irish Parliaments Between 1310 and 1800

ISBN/EAN: 9783744734448

Printed in Europe, USA, Canada, Australia, Japan

Cover: Foto ©ninafisch / pixelio.de

More available books at **www.hansebooks.com**

HISTORY OF IRELAND,

AS DISCLOSED ~~BY~~

IRISH STATU~~TES~~

PASSED BY

IRISH PARLIAMENTS BETWEEN 1310 AND 1800.

BY

A. M. ROWAN.

LONDON:
PRINTED AND PUBLISHED FOR THE
CONSERVATIVE CENTRAL OFFICE,
ST. STEPHEN'S CHAMBERS, WESTMINSTER, S.W.
BY
THE NORTH LONDON ECHO COMPANY, LIMITED, WOOD GREEN, N.

Price, paper covers, 1s. 1d.; cloth, 2s.

Dedicated
TO
R. M. LITTLER, C.B., Q.C.,
WHOSE CONVERSATION FIRST SUGGESTED, AND WHOSE KIND SYMPATHY HAS ENCOURAGED, THE WORK OF PREPARING THIS SYNOPSIS OF THE STATUTES OF THE OLD IRISH PARLIAMENT.

PREFACE.

THIS little book needs a few words of preface. It has been put hastily together, with a view of showing how turbulence in Ireland has been fostered since "the coming of the English"; how in early days "settled" English and Irish made laws to protect themselves from being "preyed" upon by the "unsettled" English and Irish who swarmed outside the pale of this growing civilisation; how "alien" clerical Romish interference had to be curtailed in *lay matters* by the earlier settlers in Ireland, who themselves had planted that "alien" church in Ireland; how religious bigotry grew up amongst us. The Act of Richard II. against the Romish clerical misdoers, being revived by Philip and Mary to "suppress" Protestants; this same Act being used afterwards by Elizabeth and put in force against "papists."

Thus religious differences, created about the time of Henry VIII., grew into the religious hate of the seventeenth and eighteenth centuries, and are the root of the religious jealousy of to-day. "Racial hate," as now described, is of even a more recent date amongst us. This took its start from the sixteenth century, when the Desmonds and Ormonds English settlers proved themselves more Irish than the Irish, repudiating the laws established for the King's subjects, and reverting to those Irish Brehon laws, which gave them—by reason of "the strong hand" more wealth and power.

From first to last the " intention " of the laws was to " protect " the " settled " and suppress the turbulent people in Ireland. That the means adopted did not accomplish the end desired, is made apparent by the continual recurrence of "rebellions." The legislation of those days was undoubtedly partial, and, though evidently carefully prepared to meet existing "grievances," was somewhat short-sighted and one-sided: moreover there certainly was considerable maladministration. That maladministration was often the result of unavoidable ignorance on the part of those in office, who were guided by untrustworthy information supplied by corrupt, suborned or interested persons.

It is clearly demonstrated that after "rebellions" resulting in confiscation of lands, much care was taken to "restore" and "settle" the land question. That in thus "settling" and "restoring," great care was taken not to disturb those planted during the rebellious period is evident. That where State policy compelled the removal of such planters the State gave them compensation for such disturbance is clearly proved. Also, that where late owners were "restored" (none being restored who were not proved to be innocent), they were generally prevented by the act of restoration from *disturbing* those *planted on their lands,* being themselves "restored" to other vacant lands, or given money in lieu of the "planted" lands. It is worthy of note by those now endeavouring to "resettle" Irish lands, that only in exceptional cases were the "restored" persons permitted to re-occupy lands which were "planted."

I think there are few actual mistakes in this brief sketch of the Irish Statutes of the Irish Parliaments—Parliaments which, be it remembered, were in the early days open to Irish representatives, and until the religious feud arose, composed entirely of Roman Catholics, and for many years after free to both religions, the Religious Disability Bill being of quite recent date.

At no time, until Grattan's Parliament, excepting in what are styled "rebel" Parliaments whose Acts were not considered constitutional, was the Irish Parliament "independent" of the control of the English Parliament.

Though free of mistakes as to facts, I am aware there are many literary and other blemishes. Had time permitted, I should have endeavoured to correct these. As it is, I excuse myself to the readers on account of the haste with which this little book is compiled.

The idea of putting forward the old Irish Statutes as an argument against forming a new Home Rule Parliament, was only suggested so recently as last August. Since then I have gone through all the Irish Statute Books from 1314 to 1800, and selected Acts which illustrate the tendency of the seven periods into which this book is divided. The first six periods mark the growth of constitutional law out of chaos. The seventh is the completion of the conflict between mere brute force and educated reason in the governing of Ireland.

With all its imperfections this summary of Irish History, as shown by Irish Statutes and other cotemporary evidences, is sent out to the world in the hope of convincing thoughtful readers that it is not by such a retrograde movement as another Irish Parliament, but by a firmer consolidation of the united interests of England and Ireland, that Ireland will be improved and "settled," her best National instincts developed, and those great civil and religious rights which we now enjoy be secured. We, in Ireland, feel that by a further knitting of our interests with England, the great power for good, and vast commercial interests of *our Empire*, will be enlarged, and that together the nationalities which have created and now compose the British Empire can best withstand the assault of external enemies or internal strifes.

A. M. ROWAN.

TRALEE,
November 14*th*, 1892.

AN INTRODUCTION

TO THE

IRISH STATUTES.

I HAVE ventured to place as an introduction to the "Irish Statutes" an old MS., because it explains clearly about the English who first came into Ireland, the state of Ireland up to the middle of the sixteenth century, and shows good and sufficient reasons for the severity of some of the earlier Irish Statutes. It tells in brief but realistic words how, forgetting that their mission in Ireland was to inculcate law and order, the English themselves were the leaders of rebellion; how, upon finding that by adopting Irish customs and following the Brehon law, they could more easily acquire power and wealth, they repudiated the king's law and "preyed" upon the more orderly inhabitants of the country. Moreover, I do so with pleasure, as this paper exculpates "the Irish" from the generally received opinion of *their* being always in a state of disaffection and rebellion.

IRELAND, AS DESCRIBED BY LAWRENCE NOWEL, DEAN OF LICHFIELD, WHO DIED 1576.

This Portion was Recently Copied from a MS. (Domitian A. 18) in the British Museum.

AN ABBREVIATION OF THE GETTING OF IRELAND TO THE DECAY OF THE SAME.

Ireland of the old time had five Kings. One of Leinster which containeth five counties. . . .

Munster, which hath two portions, one by south the river of Shenin from Waterford to Limerick containing five counties, that is to say Waterford, Cork, Kerry, Tipperary and Limerick. The second by west called Briens country or Thomar (Thomond).

And the County of Connaught containing six counties . . .

Ulster containeth counties ten. . . .

The chief of these five Kings (called the monarch) kept the County of Meath with himself *ad mensa*. that is for the maintenance of his more honourable diet.

The most part of Leinster, Connaught, South Munster, Meath and Ulster was conquered by King Henry II., Empriss, and by the Lords and gentlemen coming into Ireland by his licence and commandment. The chief was Richard Erl of Strongbo, who married McMurroghs daughter, by which, as well as by MacMurghowes gift as by Conquest, he enjoyed all Leinster, and brought it to good order and obedience of the Kings law. He enjoyed it eight years during McMurghowes life and six years after in his owne. He died fourteen years after the conquest leaving but one daughter whom the King married to William erl Marshall, who came into Ireland and enjoyed all Leinster sixty years after the conquest and left it obedient to the Kings laws at his death. *Except* certain of the blood of McMurghowe whom he suffered because of him (McMurghowe) within the dwelling in the county of Caterlagh, in a place as it were a

Jerony casie I VIt'o This Erl had issue by his wife five Sons and five daughters. The Sons were Erls of Leinster the one after the other and ruled it in peace and obedience during all their lives which continued to the time of Edward the first (1272). The five daughters were all married in England to Lords who after the death of their brethren divided Leinster amongst them. The eldest had the County of Caterlagh. The Second Wexford. The third Kilkenny. The fourth Kildare, the fifth the manor of Dunamah in Leis with other certain lands in the county of Kildare.

The Lords their husbands having great possessions in England of their own, regarded little the defence of land in Ireland; but took the profits thereof, for a while as they could, and some of them never saw the land at all. And when the revenues began to decay he that had Dunamah in Leis *retained an Irishman*, one of the Mores, to be his captain in Leis, in defence thereof. The others that had Wexford and Caterlagh retained one of the Kavanaghs, that remained in Idrone, to be his Captain, taking no regard to dwell there themselves; so that within twenty years after, or thereabouts, in the beginning of Edward the Second's time, More that was Captain of Leis, kept that portion as his own, calling himself O'More. And the others of the Kavannaghs kept a great piece of the counties of Caterlagh and Wexford, calling himself M'Morghowe.*

And within little space McMurghowe growing in strength raised the Birnes and Thohiles (O'Tooles?) in his aid, so that hitherto they have kept all the country betwixt Caterlagh and the East Sea as their own. Which is thirty miles and more, and so began the decay of Leinster. The successors of this McMuroghowe being in strength in the latter end of King Edward the third's days, recieved of the King as wages [for keeping the peace?—A. M. R.] eighty marks yearly out of the exchequer.

It is to be considered, and true it is, that every of the five portions that were conquered by the King and nobles, left under tribute certain Irishmen of principal blood of their nation, who were before the Conquest inhabitants of the land. In Leinster Kavannagh of the blood of MacMuroghowe. In South Munster the McArties of the blood of McArtic sometime King of Cork. In West Munster where OBrine is, which I reade was never conquered nor obedient to the Kings laws. OBrine and his blood have continued there still, who bare tribute to Henry the Second and his Successors by the space of 100 years.

* This is the period, 1310, when the first Irish parliament was called.—A.M.R.

And the lord Cuthbert de Clare, erl of Gloucester, had one of the best manors in OBryens country, and dwelled therein.

In Connaught were left certain of the blood of OConor, sometime King thereof, and certain of the OKelleyes and others. In Ulster certain of the Neles, of the blood of ONele, Sometime King thereof. In Meath certain of the blood of OMalaghlin sometime king thereof and divers others.

All these Irishmen have ever since been inclined to English rule and order; waiting ever *when Englishmen would rebel and digress from obedience of laws which,* (*more harm is*) *have fallen to the purpose* as hereafter shall be more plainly declared.

All the South portion of Munster, betwixt Waterford and Limerick were conquered by King Henry the Second and the nobles who inhabited the Same. The Geraldines, the Butlers, the Roens, Barries and Cogans, with many others, so that it was English and obedient to the lawes the space of 160 years, as it appeareth by the Kings records. In King Edward the thirds days Lionel duke of Clarence, lieutenant of Ireland, perceeving not only that the lords of Munster, but also of other countrys, began to incline to Irish rule and order; at a parliament holden at Kilkenny made certain statutes for the Common wealth, and for the preservation of English order, which if they had been put in use the people had hitherto been obedient to the Kings laws. These were called the statutes of Kilkenny, which were these.

1. No man should take coyne ne livery upon the King's Subjects, which would destroy hell itself if they were used in the same.

2. None of the King's English subjects should make any alliance by attirage or fosterage with any of the Irish nation.

3. No man of the Kings English subjects [possessed of lands and tenements.—A. M. R.] should marry any woman Irish, or woman man upon pain of forfeiture of all their lands. With divers other beneficial statutes for the maintenance of English order.

So long as these statutes were observed the land prospered and obeyed the Kings law. But soon after the dukes departure into England, the great lords, as well of Munster as of Leinster, being in great wealth and growing into great name and authority, as John FitzThomas, lately created Erl of Kildare, James Butler then created Erl of Ormond (being divided amongst themselves) began to make alterage with Irishmen for their strength to resist others, and distained to take punishment of knights being the Kings justices or deputies for the time. By reason whereof the Erls of Ormond and of Desmond, by strength of Irishmen on either side, fought together a battle in King Henry the Sixths time wherein all the good men of the town of Kilkenny, with many others, were slain. Since which time (1422) neither the Geraldines of Munster have obeyed the Kings law, but continually allied themselves with Irishmen. Using coyne and livery whereby all the land is now of Irish rule, except the little English pale within the counties of Dublin, Meath and Uriel, which pass not three or forty miles in length.

In this manner, for lack of punishment of these great lords of Munster, by want of ministration of justice by their extortions of coyne and livery, and by other abuses, they have expelled all the English freeholders, and inhabitants out of Munster, so that in fifty years passed was none there obedient to the kings laws, except in cities and towns. Which thing hath been the decay of Munster.

The Countye of Meath was given by Henry the second to Sir Hugh de Lacie, to hold of the King by knights service. For which Sir Hugh conquered the same and gave much of it to lords and gentlemen to hold of him. And as he was building the Castle of Dernath in West Meath, he was traiterously slain by a mason of his own, as it is written in the Chronicles q^d *ibi cessavit conquesta Hyberniæ.*

He left two sons, Sir Walter and Sir Hugh. Sir Walter dying left two daughters. The elder was married to Sir Theobald de Verdun, the other to Geoffrey Prinville who departed Meath betwixt them. Sir Geoffrey had the manor of Trim, to whom the King is heir. The manor of Logsedie came in Theobalds portion, who had none heir but daughters which were married in England to the Lord Furnival and others who dwelled still in England. Taking such profits as they could get for a while, and sent small defence therefor, so that within few years all was lost. Except certain manors within the English pale which Thomas baron of Slane and Sir Robert Holywood, Sir John Crucc and Sir John Bellewe *purchased* in King Richard the Second his day's. And thus decayed the half of Meath which obeyed not the Kings laws these hundred years.

In Connaught Cuthbert de Clare, Erl of Gloucester, Sir William Bourg and Sir William Byrningham of Annery, under Henry the Second, were principal conquerors thereof. And with their Captains inhabited the Same, made it English abd obedient to the laws from OBrynes country to Sligo, in length about sixty miles. Which continued so 160 years to King Edward the thirds days. The decay whereof shall appear in Ulster.

Sir John Courcey, under Henry the Second was chief conqueror of Ulster, who therein fought Seven battles with the Irishmen, whereof he has won five and lost two. Nevertheless he got it and brought it to English rule and order, and so continued about twenty years; until King John having him in displeasure for certain evil reports that he should have made of him for killing his elder brother Geoffrey's son, wrote into Ireland to Sir Walter de Lacie and to his brother Sir Hugh, to take the said Courcey and send him into England to execution. Wherefor Hugh went into Ulster with an army, and fought with him a battle at Downe, where many were slain and Courcey obtained the victory. Which done Sir Hugh practised with certain of Courcey's men to betray their master for money. Whereby on the Good Friday ensuing he took the said Courcey going about the churchyard of Downe. He paid the traitors for their labour as he promised, hanging them up incontinently according to their deserts. The King gave to Sir Hugh for this service the Erldom of Ulster, who enjoyed it during his life and died leaving one only daughter who was married to Sir Walter De Burg lord of Connaught, so that he was erl of Ulster and lord of Connaught and enjoyed them both long time in obedience. His son Sir William de Burg did also the like, and likewise his son Sir Richard who might spend yearly £1000 ster. and above. He had issue John, which John had issue William, which William had issue but one daugher. He was traiterously slain by his own men. His daughter was married to Lionel duke of Clarence, who held the same in peace and obedience so long as he tarried in Ireland, which was not long.

At his departure he left small defence in both places, so that in King Richard's days certain knights of the Burg brethern, kinsmen of the lord William, who during his life had the rule of Connaught, in his absence, considering themselves far from punishment, and their lord out of the land, usurped all the country to themselves. Making daly alliance and friendship with Irishmen, they fell to Irish orders; so, that the Duke being dead, his heir had never any revenue out of Connaught. And so for lack of looking to and defence, not only that, but also Ulster, before King Edward the fourths day, who was true heir thereunto, was lost. So that at this day the King hath no profit at all therein, Saving only the manor of Carlingford. So thus are decayed, for lack of good defence, both Connaught and Ulster.

Some men be of opinion that the land is harder to be reformed, than it was at the first to be conquered. Considering that Irishmen have more hardyness and policy in war, more harness and artillery than they had at the conquest. To this may be shortly answered, that, surely Irishmen have not such wisdom nor policy, but English-

wen, setting themselves thereto, will far exceed them. And as for
large and small artillery, therein we excel them by far, and as for
horsemen, I have had experience that in all my days I never
found that 100 footmen or horsemen of Irish would abide to fight
with so many English. Whereof I report me to the Duke of Norfolk
and others that have been there. Another advantage is, that at the
Conquest there were not in Ireland five castles nor piles out of the
cities, and now there be 500 Castles and piles.

The four Saints of Ireland, St. Patrick, St. Columbe, St. Braghan,
St. Maling prophisied many hundred years ago, that Englishmen
should Conquer Ireland, and keep it in propriety so long as they
should keep their own laws, but falling into Irish order they should
decay.

The beginning of reformation should be in Leinster Situated in
an angle betwixt Waterford and Dublin. Wherein no Irishmen
should dwell, but the Kavannaghs, of whom McMuroghowe is
captain which cannot make 200 horse, and the Birnes and Theohills
which cannot make 100, besides the Irish of the country which
be but used men and kerne.

To help on one side of them is Wexford, English, on the other
Kildare and Dublin, on the west Kilkenny or Kilbegs, notably
Dunbrothie and Tintern in Wexford, Saradowsk, Caterlagh, Crane,
Ballylanke in Kildare.

To be given, old Ross with the Sasagh of Beautrime, the Castle of
Caterlagh, the manor of Rathvill and Clonmore, the Lordship of
Wexford, the Castle of Ferns, the Abbey of Dowskleghlin, Baltinglas
and Crane, Castle Kevine, the manor of Rathdowne and Powerscourt,
the castles of Wicklow and Arklow, the castles of Attree and Wood-
stock, with the barony of Reban to stop OMore from Kildare. The
manor of Rahangan to stop OConor. The castles of McMurghowes
country and OBirns.

[Here follow a list of all the churches and church dignitaries then in
Ireland. A.M.R.]

A DESCRIPTION OF THE POWER OF IRISHMEN.

None of this land obey the Kings laws, saving a part of the four
Shires called Meath, Uriel, Dublin and Kildare, which of their own
power be scant able to maintain the war of the Irish. Ireland
was of old divided into 5 portions called Cowiges—Leinster, both
Mesters—Desmond and Thomond—Connaught and Ulster.

LEINSTER.

McMurghowe is prince of Leinster. He and his kinsmen will be 200 horse well harnessed, a battle of Caloglas, and 300 kerns of his country Idrone.

OBirn, lord of Ybrannagh	60 horse,	1 battll.	88 kern.	
OThohil, of Fereevolin and Ymale	24 „	1 „	80 „	
Art MacDonogho, lord of Ykonsesy	16 „	— „	60 „	
Redmond MacShane, lord of Gowlbraml	8 „	— „	40 „	
O'Morghowe, lord of Yphelimi	16 „	— „	40 „	
O'Nowlane, lord of Tohyrly	12 „	— „	20 „	
OBrenan, lord of Yolongh	— „	— „	40 „	
O'More, Lord of Leis	60 „	1 „	200 „	
O'Riane, Lord of	12 „	„	24 „	
McGilpatrick, lord of Ossirie	40 „	1 „	60 „	
McMorrish, of Yury	6 „	— „	24 „	
O'Dunn, lord of Yregar	8 „	— „	200 „	
O'Demsy, lord of Chirvalire	24 „	— „	100 „	
O'Conar, lord of Ophaly	60 „	1 „	200 „	

Suma—260 horse; 5 battll. of Caloglas; 1508 kerns.

Wexford 60 horse and 200 kern, so environed with Irishmen that they cannot answer the Kings deputy; neither have power to keep themselves, *save only by paying yearly tribute to Irishmen.*

The Butlers in Kilkenny 80 horse, 2 battles, 200 kern. The Geraldines of Munster environed with Irish hardly can keep themselves.

The County of Catherlagh without aid not able to keep itself and was lately conquered by the erl of Kildare.

DESMOND.

McArtie More, Prince and lord of that portion of his own name	40 horse,	2 battll.	2000 kern.	
McArtie Reagh, lord of Carberry	60 „	1 „	2000 „	
McDonogh McArtie, Lord of Aballie	24 „	1 „	200 „	
O'Kien, Lord of	22 „	„	100 „	
O'Crowlie, Lord of	8 „	„	60 „	
O'Downeghuan, Lord of	6 „	„	60 „	
O'Flydriseol, Lord of Corelagh and Baltimore, who useth long galop	6 „	— „	200 „	
O'Maghond, lord Fousheragh	16 „	— „	120 „	

Sullivan Berne . . .	16 horse,	batt ll.	200 kern.
O D... w , Chaulligh	6 ,,	,,	60 ,,
M Gil.. Idie, Lord of	— ,,	,,	110 ,,
O'C nor Kirrie	21 ,,	,,	120 ,,
A sep' of t e Brienes dwelling at the man r f Cai r	20 ,,	,,	60 ,,
Another sept at Ilaerila h . .	8 ,,	,,	24 ,,
Other of them in the Combraghes	6 ,,	— ,,	24 ,,

Soma — 304 horse; 5 battle; 5648 kierne.

The Erl of Desmond and his kin hath of lands under him 120 miles. Four hundred horse, eight battles of Galoglas, 1 battalion crossbow men and gunners, three thousand kerns. His country is l ng, and so environed, and hateth the kings laws, so they give none ai l. A part of Burghs, called the Bourgh country, twenty four horse, one battalion, two hundred kern environed and dissevered. Part of the Butlers in Tipperary, sixty horse, two battalions, two hundre l kern. Severed amongst themselves and enemies, and environe l.

THOUMOUND.

O'Brien, lord of Thoumonnd .	200 horse,	2 battalions,	600 kern.
McNemarry, lord of Clinchollan .	200 ,,	1 ,,	600 ,,
McMahowne, lord of Corke [unintelligible] . . .	20 ,,	— ,,	60 ,,
O'Conor, lord of Corcunree .	24 ,,	— ,,	100 ,,
O'Dall, lord of Yfermghe . .	8 ,,	— ,,	24 ,,
O'Loghlin, lord of Borin . .	20 ,,	— ,,	100 ,,
O'Br n Aragh, of the Brenes Lord of Aragh . . .	40 ,,	1 ,,	100 ,,
McBren, lord of Konagh .	16 ,,	— ,,	60 ,,
O'Mulrian, lord of M ng .	24 ,,	— ,,	100 ,,
M Teg, lord of one of the Ormonds	24 ,,	- ,,	60 ,,
O'K nely, lord of the other Ormond	60 ,,	1 ,,	120 ,,
O'Caree, lor l of Ely . . .	80 ,,	16 ,,	140 ,,
O'Maghir, lord of l. Kerrin . .	16 ,,	— .	100 ,,
O'Dwire, lord of Kilnemanagh .	12 ,,	— ,,	100 ,,
McTieg McPhilip, lord of Kalend longict	6 ,,	— ,,	40 ,,

Soma — 150 horse; Caloglas, 6 battalion; 2144 kern.

IRISH STATUTES, 1310—1800. 13

CONNAUGHT.

O'Conor Downe, Lord thereof with his kin	120 horse,	2 battalions,	300 kern.
O'Conaghor Downe, lord of Maghir Conaght			
O'Conaghor Rowe			
O'Kellie, lord of Ymany	200 „	2 „	400 „
O'Flahirty, lord of Tharconaght	11 „	— „	100 „
O'Mayle, lord of Owhmale [O'Malley (?)]	16 „	— „	200 „

Long Galleys.

O'Gara, lord of Kowlowine	14 „	— „	100 „
O'Flarrty Buy, lord of Lince	6 „	— „	100 „
O'Dowde, lord of Tirgheragh Moy	20 „	— „	300 „
O'Shaghnesse, lord of Kmealeagh	12 „	— „	40 „
O'Madden, lord of Shilangee	14 „	— „	110 „
McDonogho, lord of Tyurris, *alias* Timical	40 „	1 „	160 „
McDermoth, lord of Moylorg	40 „	1 „	200 „
McManishy, Yoonghur, lord of Charbrey	40 „	1 „	200 „
O'Ruork, lord of one of the Brennes	40 „	1 „	300 „
Magranel, lord of Montirosh	8 „	— „	300 „
Magauran, lord of Taliagha	6 „	— „	200 „
O'Faral, lord of Analy	60 „	1 „	300 „
O'Raylie, lord of the other Brennes	60 „	1 „	400 „

Suma—868 horse; 10 battalions; 3740 kern.

McWilliam Bourg, lord of Clanricard severed	120 horse,	2 batts.,	300 kern.
McWilliam Bourg, called McWilliam Eughter, lord of Keniketche	200 „	3 „	300 „
The Lord Birmingham, lord of Konnikedon, nere	14 „	— „	40 „
Nangle, lord of Clyncosteh	12 „	— „	40 „
McShertane, called Depher, lord of Gallin	12 „	— „	60 „
McKemill, lord of Kerr	— „	— „	160 „
McDavil Bourg, lord of Clinkene	24 „	— „	40 „
McPhelippim Bourg, lord of Oyel	— „	— „	40 „

I=th the said Lord Bourgh, called either of them McWilliam, be
most of enemies, and the Irishmen be severed with them, and will be
of no better condition than Irishmen, wearing Irish apparel, and so
intended and allied with them, that they take their part against the
Kings subjects, hating the Kings laws.

ULSTER.

O'Neil, lord of that portion of Tyrone with his blood and kinsmen .	200	horse,	3	batt.,	300	kern.
Con McHugh Buy, lord of Clanyboy	200	„	3	„	200	„
O'Kahane, lord of Yraghticassari	60	„	1	„	100	„
McFlonye, lord of the Clinnes .	20	..		,	100	..
McGennis, lord of Iveagh.	60	„	1	„	200	„
McWilliam, lord of the Roote .	20	„			100	„
McKartane, lord of Kinalertes .	6	„		„	100	„
O'Hanlin, lord of Orir .	24	„		„	60	..
McMahon, lord of Loghther	40	„	1	„	300	„
McGwire, lord of Trughes	10	„	—	„	40	..
McKawel, lord of Kinalard	8	„		„	40	„
O'Donil, lord of Tirconel .	100	„	1	,	300	„
In the Ard dwelleth Lanago an Englishman. So environed he is almost expulsed out of the country	24	„	1	„	60	„
McMahound, Lord of Irish Uriel						

Suma—Horse, 811 ; Galoglas, 15 Batt.; Kern, 2160.

MIDTH [MEATH].

Wherein be these Irishmen, none whereof obeyeth the Kings laws.

O'Malaghlin, lord of Clincolman calling himself Prince of Meath .	24	horse,	—	batt.,	100	kern.
O'Mulmoy [Molloy], lord of Ferical	20	„	—	„	100	..
Magoghigan, lord of Kinaleagh .	24	„	—	„	80	„
Sinnagh, lord of Montirhagan .	6	„	—	„	24	„
McCawbe, lord of Katbrim	1	„	—	„	24	..
O'Brinn, lord of Brahon .	—	„	—	„	60	„
McCoglan, lord of Delha .	8	„	—	„	120	„

Suma—86 Horse ; 508 Kern.

Suma totalis—Galoglas, 41 Battalions; Horse, 3315; Kern, 15,701.

A Battallion of Galoglas 60 or 80 men harnessed, on foot, with spears, every one whereof hath his knave to bear his harness, whereof some have spears, some have bows.

Every Kern hath a bow, a skein or three spears, a sword or a skein, without harness, and every two have a lad to bear their gear.

Every horseman hath two horses. Some three, a Jack well harnessed, for the more part a sword, a skein, a great spear and a dart. Every horse hath a knave, and their chief horse is ever lead, and one of his knaves ride always and bear his harness and spears, if he have harness.

They be for the most part good and hardy men of war, and can live hardly and suffer great misery. They will adventure themselves greatly on their enemies, seeing time to do it. Good watchers in the night, as good soldiers by night as others by day. These Irishmen hate the Kings laws and subjects mortally. And notwithstanding all gifts and other help, when they see time they do their best for their own advantage.

They used always to make themselves strong, and all the goods of their subjects they take when it pleases them as their proper goods.

When a lord dieth the strongest and best is made lord after him, and captain, and seldom doth any of the sons succeed his father.

They get many children besides [those of] their wives, whereof all be gentlemen, and their fathers lands purchased and farms is equally divided amongst them.

Their sons learn to be men of war from the age of 16 years, and be continually practised in the toyles thereof.

They provide for the beneficcs from Rome though they can scarcely read, *the profits whereof they spend against us.* But God provideth. Setting continual dissension amongst them and mortal wars.

PACES TO BE CUT [Roads made?].

Down Calliber, the new Dickie, the paces going to Powerscourt, Ylankrid, Belaghmore in Tendért [Clonfert], Barndarragh going to Fernslerage, Strenagloragh, Rollmontie, Brunvalle, Flangery, Mortenstown, two paces in Sleigmore, the paces of Farranobeghan, Killemartethe, Bellanower, Logher Neson, two paces in Katra [Cultra], the pace of Brahon, Turin, Kilkoykie, the Lagher and Rettrae, Karriconall and Belaghmore, three paces in Orore, Ornby, Donghele, the other by Faghirt, the third by Omee [Omagh] Belaghkine and Belaghmore.

James of Desmond, Grandfather to the lord that now is, about they ye... ... put first coyne and livery on the Kings subjects in his country, whom the rest followed until all was come to naught, the [Brehon] laws being exiled, and the subjects no better than his men.

The Erl of Ulster might dispend above 30,000 marks by the year, having under him five shires besides other lordships, the counties of Lowbrough, Antrim, Cragfergus, Newton and Lecale.

The abominable use of Coyne and livery was brought into the four English counties, Meath, Louth, Dublin and Kildare by James Fitz of Desmond son to the aforesaid James, *being then deputy*, and was put to death therefor.

Then ensued Coyne and livery, Boone Cuddwe, Carliggeariages, Journeys and other impositions. Whereas in some places thirty years ago were six bows [men] now is not one.

THE REVENUES OF IRELAND.

A Battalion town containeth 960 acres of arable land, besides woods, moors and pastures.

Leinster containeth	31	Cantreds	Batayle towns.		
Ulster	„	35	„	i	930 bet.
Desmond	„	35	„	i	1050 „
Thomound	„	35	„	i	1050 „
Connaught	„	35	„	i	900 „

Both the Brienies, i Breny ORurk and Breny O'Reily were not counted in Connaught at that time,

Which contain	400 bet.
Meath containeth 18 Cantreds i	540 „

It was at that time from the water of Alef to the water of Down-doughere. *Suma totalis* of Batayle towns 5920. This division was made before the conquest, wherefore now it is more one penny of every acre of land, amounts to yearly, to the sum of £24,900.

The inheritance of the Captains in Ireland goeth not by succession, but by election and *forte main*, so that he who is strongest ever succeedeth. By reason whereof there is almost always rebellion against the Lord.

The captain or lord keepeth none of his lands in his own hands, but giveth it to his followers, by whom he is maintained in all things necessary or what it pleaseth him to take, for all that they have is at his command.

Some call them Isages, *i.e.* Dukes.
The Englishmen become Irishmen be these.
The Erl of Desmond.
The Knight of Kerry.
Fitzmorishe Kelly, Lord Cogan.
Sir Thomas Desmond, Lord Bared.
Sir Gerald of Desmond, the White Knight.
Lord Barry, the Knight of the Vale.
Lord Roache.
Sir Gerald Desmonds Sons.
John, Lord Barry of the County Waterford.
Lord Courcy.
The Powers of the County of Waterford.
Sir William Bourg of the county Limerick.
Sir Pierce Butler, and all the Captains of the Butlers in the county of Kilkenny and Fedart.

In Connaught.

Lord Bourg of Corukeghoule.
Erl of Clanrickard.
Lord Birmingham of Auric.
Sir Miles Stauntons sons.
Sir Jordan Stauntons sons.
Lord Naugill.
Sir Walter Barretts sons.

In Ulster.

Lord Savage of Lecale.
Fitzhowten of Liskard.
FitzJohn Lissed of the Chinnes.

In Meath.

The Dillons, Daltons, Tyrolls, Dellamaris.

All the Countys of Ireland.

Waterford	Caterlagh
Cork	Uriel
Kilkenny	Meath
Limerick	Dublin
Kerry	Kildare
	Wexford.

Connaught and Ulster.

The English counties *paying yearly tribute to wild Irish* called Blackrent

The barony of Lecale to the Captain of Clandeboye	£40
The County of Uriel to ONele	£40
Meath, to O'Conor, Opholy,	£300
The county of Kildare to O'Coghnor	£20
County Wexford to McMurghowe Buy	£10
County of Kilkenny and Tipperary to O'Carril	£10
County Limerick to O'Brene	£40
The same to O'Brene, Aragh	£10
County Cork to Carmock McTeig	£40
The Exchequer to McMorghowe	80 marks

Suma totalis £710.

IRISH STATUTES.

BRIEFLY ABSTRACTED FROM IRISH PARLIAMENTARY RECORDS

1310—1800.

NOTES—PART I.

1310—1500.

THERE is a Royal Commission preparing "the antient laws of Ireland" for publication. To these we make but passing allusion, but while the Home Rule of to-day is still inchoate it is interesting to look back and see what old "Irish" Parliaments have done in the past. "Irish Parliaments," both "rebel" and otherwise, have "sat" in Ireland at various times, and in various places, ever since 1310. The Brehon, or old Irish laws, were entirely in favour of "the strong hand." It was the capricious adoption of these Brehon laws by the "settled English," when they found that by these laws they obtained more advantages over the "Irish who came in," than by the new code. Which code being in a strange tongue created first bewilderment, secondly, discontent in the mind of the "Irish who came in." The "laws," framed for "the King's subjects in Ireland," were in the English tongue, which for many, many generations the Irish did not understand; therefore they were angered to find the "law" administered by interested parties, apparently without finality and always adverse to their interests.

In those early days "the laws" were framed for "the

King's subjects in Ireland," not for a conquered people. These laws made no distinction between the "English or Irish subjects," or "the English rebels and Irish enemies of the King" in Ireland. The distinction which created the difference was made, not by "the law," but by the maladministration of that law by selfish or ignorant individuals. The differences of these early days have developed into the racial hate spoken of at the present time.

Those earlier laws were almost entirely "defensive" rules for protecting those small minorities dwelling in the "Settled Country," from the "preying of the hordes of English rebels and Irish enemies" who swarmed in the wide "unsettled" country. Later on laws were framed for protecting "the poor" from the "Comerick and Safeguard" of the rich and strong, from extortionate Church fees unlawfully claimed, and other "official perquisites" taken from "the people" by "the greater people."

Later on, for the better ordering of the country, the Irish Parliament declared all laws made in England should be "confirmed" or adopted in Ireland. This fact, and another is suggestive, namely, that very many laws initiated by Irish Parliaments and passed into law during one session were promptly repealed in the next session; until, it was ultimately "ordered" by the Irish House of Commons that "no law" should be brought before that House for consideration until it was first "approved" in England. The principle of our present law of "Compensation for Malicious Injury" is almost identical with a very old Act passed by an Irish Parliament in 1465; while the promptness with which "rents" were exacted in those days is in striking contrast with the indulgent proceedings of 1892. These earlier "law-makers" recognised that the essence of good government was to protect the weak from the tyranny of the strong; but their "laws," read to-day in the brighter light of a wider experience and larger knowledge of the laws of nature and political economy, show them inadequate and unsuited for attaining that desired end. Up to 1800 the governors of Ireland were apparently endeavouring to accomplish a delicate job with very inefficient instruments and thus to have created many miseries.

THE PREAMBLE OF THE OLD STATUTES OF THE IRISH PARLIAMENTS.
1310—1500.

Previous to 1762, when His Excellency Lord Halifax, Lord Lieutenant of Ireland, gave order "that the Statutes at large of this kingdom be printed and published under the inspection of the Lord Chancellor and Judges," there had been no uniform "Irish Statute" book. Some statutes were only in manuscript, some were lost, while others had been printed at different times in various shapes and forms.

This edition was to be made as complete as the muniments of the nation, the care of the Lord Chancellor and Judges, and the assiduity of Francis Vesey, to whom they entrusted the editing and indexing, could make it.

The first volume commences with "Acts and Ordinances of the Parliament of Kilkenny, *Octavis Purificationis* of the Virgin Mary, in the third year of the reign of King Edward II., Anno Domini, 1310." The first Act is, to restrain great lords from "taking prizes from, or lodging or sojurning against their will, with people who tilled the soyle." Because these, merchants and others, "lesser people," suffered, owing to the way in which these lords "took all they willed" *never* "paying anie man aniething.'

The next Parliament mentioned, sat in Dublin A.D. 1429, "before the Right noble and right gracious Lord, Sir Thomas Sutton, Knight, lieutenant of our Sovereign Lord King Henry the VI. on Friday next after the Feast of All Saints." The next Parliament was called before Richard, Archbishop of Dublin, Lord Justice of Ireland, in Dublin, on Friday, the feast of St. Dunstone, when it was desired and agreed that, "all laws for the protection of property and defence thereof, be established the same as in England; secondly, that "Comrick and Safe guard" be abolished, and "such as adopt it be deemed traitors." "Comrick and Safe guard" being a "black mailing" of His Majesty's subjects by "thieves, robbers, and rebels" who then gave these subjects "Comrick," which was protection from other "thieves," to the "discreding of the Government." The next Parliament was held at *Trymme*, the Friday next after the Epiphany, before John Earl of Shrewsbury, A.D. 1447, when an Act was passed that none of the King's liege men, or officers of his land in Ireland, may be absent from Ireland, "unless *by command, without forfeiting land and property*." Another Act, "an Englishman shall have no hair on his upper lip ... the said lip shall be shaven at least once a fortnight ... any found amongst the English contrary hereunto, that then it shall be lawful to every man to take them and their goods as Irish enemies, and to ransome them as Irish enemies." (This law was not repealed until 11 Charles 1.) Another Act was passed prohibiting "clipped money, called O'Reyles money, and other unlawful money. And against gilt bridles, peytrels, and other gilt harness, excepting for Knights and prelates of holy churches." Another Act ordered "sons of labourers and husbandmen" to follow their fathers' business. "If any do otherwise he shall be imprisoned for one year," also "make fine to the King, or lord of the Franchise, according to the discretion of the Judge before whom he is convicted." Again another Act: "Whereas this land of Ireland is greatly impoverished from day to day by the great deduction . . . and carrying out of Ireland into England . . . Silver plate, broken silver, bullion and wedges of silver, made of the great tonsure of the money of our Sovereign Lord the King, by his *Irish enemies and English rebels* within the land . . . and O'Reyles money do increase every day unto the hurt and impoverishment of the people." . . . Twelve pence for custom ordered to be paid on every ounce so removed.

The next meeting is called a "Great Council" "holden in Dublin the Friday next before the Feast of St. Luke the Evangelist, before Richard Duke of York, the King's lieutenant of Ireland, A.D. 1450. 1st Act—"That no merchant or other man keep more horsemen or footmen than they shall answer for, and maintain upon their own charges and their tenants." They must "present the names of their men," and, they *must not* take "coynees, cuddies, suppers or pledges, from the "poor husbands and tenants on the land of Ireland." For these said "Irish and English" "oppress and destroy them." By day and night they come and "spoyl" "the English country"—if allowed to go unpunished it will be "the utter destruction and undoing of the said land."

In this same year a Parliament was holden at Drogheda, the Friday next before the "Feast of St. Mark the Evangelist," before the same Duke of York. Here an Act was passed that no one should sell beer, wine or other liquor, except by "the Kings measure"—gallon, pottle, quart, pint—under a fine of forty shillings.

In 1454 another Parliament was called, before Edward Fitz Eustace, Knight, deputy of the Duke of York, when it was ordered *at the request of the Commons*, "that diverse laws" against "provisours" (who were priests), as in England so in Ireland, "against all them that sue provisions to the Court of Rome," be kept in force. Another Act makes fathers answerable for their sons and "wage men," in all but crimes answerable with death. This Parliament was followed in 1445 by another "Grand Council," wherein the Recorders of Dublin and Drogheda were ordered, because of the increasing poverty created by the aforesaid Irish enemies and English rebels, to charge only twopence for a copy of a plaint; if they took more they were "outlawed" and "out of the protection of the King."

The next Parliament assembled at Naas on the Friday next after All Saints, before Thomas Fitz Maurice Earl of Kildare, deputy to Richard Duke of York, A.D. 1457. In this Parliament persons not "amesenable" to law, entered lands without licence, killed and threatened tenants, "so that said tenants dared not dwell in the lands, but must fly . . . and leave them waste, which is a great mischief, like to make much of this land waste . . . such 'amensable' persons out of (outside) the law, at this day have more great rule, for default of punishment of misgovernance, than persons that obey the law . . . so they (that do so) shall lose their title and claim to said land for ever to them and their heirs." In conclusion, "*this statute shall not extend to such persons as are amensable to the common law.*"

Next Parliament at Dublin, Friday next after the Purification of our Lady, before Thomas Earl of Kildare, deputy to Richard Duke of York, etc., 1458, wherein an Act was passed that "all persons beneficed must keep residence"; in default "half their profits to go to the use of their churches, the other half to be spent by the King in the wars for the defence of the kingdom, "impoverished and weakened" by their absence, the "diminished service of God and withdrawing of hospitality."

This same Parliament ordered towns and villages to be enclosed, to save them from thieves who now laid them waste, roadways to be left through the villages "from one market to another."

In 1459, on the Friday next after the feast of St. Blase the Martyr, the Earl of Kildare held another Parliament in Dublin; in the following year, on the same day, one in Drogheda, in which it was ordered no one but a minister or servant to a minister of record should sue in Court of Exchequer on pain of £10.

The next Parliament was held in Dublin 1462, on the Friday next after St. Luke Evangelist, before *Rolando Fitz-Eustace* milite domino de Porttestir deputato Georgii ducis Clarenciae—Regi Ed. quarti secondo 1462—when it was ordered money received "of the issues and profits of the Courts" be spent on the repairs of the castle of the King in Dublin in which the Courts are kept. It being "ruinous and like to fall," "and that all the leads of the isles of the hall of the said castle, be sold by the treasurer of Ireland, to make and repair the said hall." The following year "*Parliament Dom' Regius apud Weys* die veneris prox' ante festum S. Martini . . . quoram Thomas Desmond . . . deput' Georgii ducis Clarenciae . . . ac abinde die Jovis, tunc prox' sequent' tenend', ac exinde die Sabbati in festum sancti Edwardi Regis, tunc prox' sequente ad villam *de Naas* . . . ad tunc prox' seq. ad civit' praed' Dom Regis *Dublin,*" etc. Because "the land was waste," destroyed "by the Irish enemies and English rebels of the King" attorneys fees were lowered for every plea twelvepence, and every copy fourpence; and if they claim more a fine of "one hundred shillings."

The next Parliament was held at Trym, on the Wednesday

next after the feast of St. Lawrence, before the Earl of Desmond, 1465.

An Act was passed thereat that any found "robbing" by day or night, or *going to rob*, unless he have in company "a faithful man of good name and fame in English apparel," may be killed, and his head brought to the portreeffe at Trim, who will give an order to the bringer to levy by his own hand twopence off every man having a ploughland, one penny off every man having a half ploughland, one penny off every man having a house worth forty shillings, and a half penny off every man having "a house and smoake," in the barony where the said thief was taken. And if the portreffe refuse the certificate he "be fined £10." Another Act provided all Irishmen in Dublin, Myeth, Uriel, and Kildare shall apparel as English men and beard like them, *swear allegiance, and take English surname*. Again, that all Irish between sixteen and sixty, that dwell with the English and speak English, be supplied with English bow and arrow. Until so supplied they get twopence a month. Another Act, that in every town they have butts to shoot at, and all practise together every holiday, "three times up and down" betwixt the "1st of March and last of July," on penalty of one halfpenny each day. Another Act was passed that no ship or vessel of any foreign country fish *in these lands* without special licence from the King; that those who do come pay thirteen and fourpence a year, or else forfeit their ship: "the north part of Wicklow is free."

In 1467 a Parliament sat in Dublin before Johanne Com' Wigorn' (no day given), wherein an Act was passed that, in future, "none purchase benefices from Rome."

"Wheras at ancient times all manner of vicars, having competent benefices did keep hospitality to the honour of God, and to the profit of the poor people, and now of late diverse men of the holy Church, suing to the Court of Rome, hath purchased Bulls from the Holy Father the Pope to have as well abbeys, priories and other dignities as parsonages and vicarages *in commendam* to the final extinguishment of divine service and hospitalities . . . whereupon . . . in eschewing of those mischiefes . . . it is enacted and established by authority of the Said Parliament, that whatsoever maner of man of holy church, purchase any manner of dignity parsonage or vicarage, by bulls of the Pope, to hold *in commendam*, except that they be out of the protection of the King, shall forfeit the value of the said benefices during his life natural . . . and shall incur in all penalties . . . made against provisors of benefices . . . it shall be lawful to the King to present to said benefices for that time, and as often as the case require aforesaid."

In 1468 a Parliament sat at Drogheda, where it was enacted that all statutes and acts made by the English Parliament " should be confirmed," and " adjudged of force in Ireland." There was also a law passed to prevent those having corn to " granell up the same to sell upon a dearth " ; or, to buy up in one market and sell " more deer " by " two or fourpence the bushel " in another market, to the " hurt of the poor."

In 1472, at Naas, a Parliament was held before the Earl of Kildare, which is the first Parliament in which the word to " prorogue " is used. In these days, " Ulster men " were taking goods out of the kingdom into Scotland, without paying " cocket " or customs to the King. They were to be tried for so doing by " 12 men of the *next adjoining county*," by the " common law," and to forfeit such goods to the King. Another law obliged all merchants to bring into Ireland, with any merchandize value a hundred pounds, " bows and arrows " to the value of a hundred shillings ;

and "so following up to twenty pounds"; if not, they were to be fined their value. It was also ordered, no grain to be taken out of Ireland when the price was "above 10*l.* per peck," on pain of forfeiture of the grain and the ship which carried it.

Again, in 1478, a Parliament was called when an Act was passed that, as "lords spiritual and temporal, and free tenants," were hurt and put to delay by "losses of their rents"; as, when "distresses" were taken they died, or "were taken" from "the pound"; it was therefore decreed, if rent were not paid within eight days, the goods be appraised by four men of the lordship; and, if in eight days after this, *the arrears of rent be not paid*, the lord may take the goods for his rent and damages; what is above the rent and damages to be restored to the tenant. Another Act was passed, that no one, *not beneficed, should be proctor*; no one not resident and spending forty shillings yearly should be knight of the shire or sit in Parliament.

Another Parliament was called in Dublin, in 1480, before the Earl of Kildare. Another, in 1493, before Walter Archbishop of Dublin, deputy for the Duke of Bedford wherein the "watercourses in St. Patricks Street, Dublin," were ordered to be cleansed by the inhabitants. The "said church and college is the foundation of our Lord the King, and the said church and close is scituated, and standeth in a low valley, nevertheless . . . the said dean and chapiter, fearing the violence of the waters and floods, to their great charge and cost . . . have made divers issues and gowts for the free avoidance of all such suddain floods: Also, there was of old time, and now there are, two rivers or passedges of water, one upon every side of St. Patrick Street, called the Podell, through which such waters had a lawful course . . . until now, when the inhabitants filled the said Podell by 'throwing in refuse from the houses, and by tanners making ditches to water their skinns.' Those that do such to be fined twenty shillings."

In 1495 Parliament was held at Drogheda before Edward Ponyngs, deputy for the King. The first Acts passed in an Irish Parliament, in the English language, were passed by this Parliament. The Treasurer, in Ireland, was therein ordered, henceforward "to make all officers in Ireland as in England . . . 2ndly, offices to be held only at the will of the king . . . 3rdly, because of 'haynous abusions' 'within the land of Ireland,' and 'confirmed by authority of Parliament late holden within the said land, afore Richard duke of York there, *then being in rebellion*, . . . which abusion and enormity is declared and spoken of through all Christian realms . . . that these laws (passed by the Duke of York) be revoked.'" This was followed by another Act, ordering "that *no Parliament be holden in this land until the Acts be certified into England. That all other Parliaments be void.*"

All statutes against "provisors" at Rome strengthened. The Acts of the Parliament of Kilkenny strengthened. That all subjects in Ireland, English and Irish, to have bows and arrows, to shoot at butts to be erected in every parish at the cost of the parishioners; and that constables in every parish see this carried out on "every holy day," under a penalty of twelve pence; also, each defaulting subject to pay a fine of fourpence, unless they show "reasonable cause." So that "all the commons of the said land may be able to doe the king or his lieutenant service, *for their owne defence or surety.*" According to their different stations the "subjects" (English and Irish) were supplied with different arms; "every freeholder of four pounds having "his horse, jack salett, bow and sheaf of arrows." Another of Poyning's acts, "no person take any money for the death or murder of friend or kinsman, other than the King's law will." That, when murder is committed, "hue and cry shall be levied according to the statute of Winchester." Again, it was enacted, "treason to stir the people to war against the King's authority, or *the Irish against the English.*" And, for the safety "of all the said land," the Constable of Dublin, Trym, Leiselipe, Alone, Wycklow, Greencastle, Carlingford and Crafergus be "*one born in the realm of England.*" That some former Acts being lost or mislaid, or embezzled, any now found keeping them be deemed felons; that now and henceforward all records be all lodged in the Treasury. Again, because owing to "penory," for the last twenty-four years, the lords of Parliament have not worn robes in Ireland; "and have done away the said robes, to their own dishonour and the rebuke of the whole land," that in future they wear them as in England; any failing to do so " to be specified and pay a hundred shillings unto the King."

" Any hereafter making war, breaking pace, or spoiling Irish enemies, without licence of the King to forfeit £100." Again the law strengthened against "coyn and livery." Another, forbidding the war-cries of "Cromaboo and Butleraboo," as disturbing the public peace. They may only call upon "St. George," or the name of the King of England for the time being. All Acts made in England to be used and exercised in Ireland.

The Acts made in the Parliament at Drogheda before Robert Preston, Lord of Gormanston, repealed, because "he had no manner of power by his commission to keep Parliament." All Acts made therein void.

In 1499 laws were made at Trisledermont, before Gerald Earl of Kildare, deputy-lieutenant in Ireland, which merely provide that laws made in England be " proclaymed at Dublin and Drogheda and other towns, to the intent that merchants may know what those Acts be, and the pains of the same."

In 1500 there was the last Parliament of Henry VII., which dealt principally with Customs duties.

NOTES—PART II.
1517—1635.

Between the years 1517 and 1635 the Parliaments in Ireland made vigorous efforts to improve the country by passing social measures. In the previous centuries the Acts passed were mostly for " repressing turbulent English and Irish disturbers of the public peace," little effort being made to foster or encourage trade or industry. In fact, the " settled " country being but a small portion of Ireland, laws were made principally for the preservation of those within this pale, all without that area being considered " outer barbarians."

Previous to 1517 those within the pale were obliged to " sue " their causes (when of importance) in England, which was a hardship upon the " poorer people," unable to support this "great expense and trouble "; therefore in this year they were enabled to " sue " in Ireland. Stringent laws were made against export, because " taking goods out of the country injured the poor "; Acts were also passed to prevent " idle fellows " who would not work from " preying upon those " who had goods."

From early days until 1537 " the English rebel and Irish enemies " in Ireland were continually described as " preying " upon the English " settlers " and Irish that " came in," to the destruction of the country. Up to this date there does not appear to have been any serious racial or religious antagonism, only a war of the large mass of " idle " and " dissolute " English and Irish upon these better behaved and steadier men of both nationalities, who were working together to civilise the country and improve their own condition. The very laws made then against " Lezers " would apply to the vagrant " loafers " of to-day, idleness and a lazy, happy go-lucky manner of life being then as now the habit of those who disdained to work, but to beg were not ashamed. These "lazy fellows" called themselves patriots, but were only active when disturbing the public peace. Parliaments were nomadic, held throughout the country, there being no settled "Parliament House."

Henry VIII. is believed to have been the "grabber" of churches. It is therefore worthy of note that the Irish Church property which he "appropriated" by Act of Parliament was the derelict property of absentee churchmen, which, with the lands of other lay absentee owners, were described as being "wasted" and overrun by "Irish enemies and English rebels." His Parliament also made a law prohibiting "proctors" (compelled to be priests) from taking part in any Parliament, as such "foreign" interference was mischievous. Besides, they did "obsucat" God's law for mundane purposes. Owing to these "grievances" being continually complained of, the King claimed to be "Supreme Head of the Church," and took upon himself to remedy these evils. It is evident that, having got the "faithful Lords and Commons to pass an Act of Parliament giving him an inch, the King proceeded to take an ell of power over the Church.

The laws as to labourers and husbandmen passed by Philip and Mary should be brought to the notice of the Labour Commission, and be studied by Messrs. Keir Hardie and Co.; while the crude views as to husbandry are worthy of the consideration of the Congested District Board.

In the days of Philip and Mary the abrupt reversal of the Church laws of the previous reign no doubt gave an opening for licence, and so were the cause of the gross excuses which took place. From henceforward there is parliamentary evidence of a growing religious and racial difference. It is no longer the "English rebel and Irish enemy" who are described as antagonistic to the "settled" country, but a feud between "Protestant" and "Papist," "English" and "Irish," which had to be legislated for. Philip and Mary "reversed" the Church laws of previous reigns, and reinstated the Pope in "such power" as he previously possessed, and also *revived* acts that had been previously in force for "ponyshing" of heretics.

When Elizabeth took up the reins of government, she ruled with "the strong hand." With a stern indifference to customs, she effaced old laws or made new ones, actually forcing the people of this country, whether they would or not, to work out their own social salvation. There was no compromise, those would not obey the laws were "wiped out."

In the seventeenth century James's Parliament repealed all the remaining old "penal laws" against the "Irish enemies," putting all "Irish subjects" on an equality with "English subjects in Ireland." In 1615 a Bill was passed whereby members of Parliament were paid for their services: every shire knight 13s. 4d. *per diem*; every citizen of a city being a county, 10s; every burgess representative, 6s. 8d. *per diem*. They received this pay for fourteen days before, after, and while attending in the Parliament. In the next session of the same Parliament, the House considered these fees too high, so they were cut down to half. There is nothing new under the sun; and the Radicals of to-day, in calling out for paid members, are only adopting a retrograde movement, in endeavouring to revive an Act passed nearly three hundred years ago.

In 1634 Charles I. made efforts to protect Irish farming. But, on the plea that the Irish were not trained to trade, the King, addressing his faithful Lords and Commons, advised all Irish manufactures to be discouraged, and forbid them to make broadcloth, for *fear of inconveniencing* trade by putting inferior articles into the market. It was to counteract this cloth prohibition that Lord Stafford started and fostered the Ulster linen trade.

At the opening of Parliament in 1634, Ireland appears to have risen to the top of a wave of a rude prosperity. Serjeant Eustace, being unanimously elected speaker, addressed the House in what, to modern ideas, are high-flown terms, and a rather too plentiful embroidery of Scriptural quotations.* Referring enthusiastically to the "leaps and bounds" of improvement during the previous decade, he congratulates the House on the good measures which produced such satisfactory results. But he concludes by pointing to certain dangers, which he counsels them to take "good and proper" measures for averting.

We will now take the leading measures of this period in seriatim.

IRISH STATUTES, 1517—1634.

The first Irish Parliament of Henry VIII. was held in Dublin 1517, before the Earl of Kildare, when the first law made, was, to prevent people in Ireland being vexatiously obliged to go to "great labour and expense" by having to sue their causes in England. The next Parliament was held in Dublin 1522, before Thomas Earl of Surrey, wherein a law was made that it was high treason to burn corn stacks or houses, by evil-disposed persons, "for malice, evil will, or displeasure; that they be punished accordingly, and the law saved," "to the chiefe lordes of the soyles their eschetes." Wools and flocks were not to be exported, as it made "a dearth of cloth, and idlenesse of many folkes, so that in default of labour . . . men and women have faln to theft and other misgovernance, to the desolation and ruins of this poor land." Another law provided that "if there

* *See post.*—A. M. R.

were not sufficient right persons within the four shires where the Kings law is occupied in this land" for the giving of "right verdicts," jurors properly qualified should try cases elsewhere. In 1534 a Parliament was called in Dublin before the Earl of Kildare, when an act for " lezers of corn " was brought in; because, "so many will not labour for their living . . . but lozing corn in harvest . . . they refuse money for their wage, refuse to rippn or binde corn ; to the intent the poor earth tillers should give them sheaves for their labour . . . wherefore they (have excuse to) steal corn by night and day, to the hinderance of earth tillers . . . also, the church is defrauded of the tythe of the same." "Whatever is lezed may therefore be seized and divided between the Lord of the soyle and the taker." Amongst the great Acts of this Parliament were uniting church properties, notably, by the prayer of the Prior of St. Peter and St. Paul of the Newton besides Tyrmme, incorporating therewith Galtrime, which was the "appropriation" of one Nicholas Husso, as "was given by force of a remainder of a trial, to one Peter Hussey, anncestor of the said Nicholas, whose heire the said Nicholas is." In the year "*anno regni ejusdum Domini Regis vicerimo octavo,*" a Parliament sat before Leonardo Gray, first in Dublin, in May, in Kilkenny, in July, and also at Cashel and Limerick, ending December 1537, for the attainment of the Earl of Kildare ; secondly for the Succession Act of the King and Queen Anne, when it was made "treason to utter anything to the slander or prejudice of the said (Henry VIII.) marriage or of the issue so inheritable." This Act entailed the succession,—failing males—upon "Lady Elizabeth, now princess . . . as the crown of England hath been accustomed and ought to go." Because of "the mischiefrs, occasioned by the absence of persons having land in Ireland," a law was made that the King enjoy all lands, castles, monasteries, etc., *so neglected*. The "winning" of these lands " in the beginning " " not onely cost the Kings noble progenitors charges inestimable, but also that to whom the land was given, then and many years after abiding in the land, nobly . . . defending the same against the Kings enemies, and, also kept the same in such tranquilitie and good order, so as the . . . laws (there were) obeyed . . . revenues paid . . . as within the realm of England . . . (now) not pondering, no regarding . . . towns, castles . . . appertaining unto them, fell into decai . . . and the English inhabitants there . . . (thus neglected) 'by compulsion of those of the Irishry were exiled,' the rebels thus are attaining the property and neglecting the King's law; therefore the King appropriates the lands of the lords and clerics, who, neglecting Ireland, went to live on their English estates." Amongst those so appropriated were Howard's (the Duke of Norfolk's), Talbot's (the Earl of Waterford's) lands, also those of the " heires general " of the " Abbot of Furnes, St. Augustins of Bristow, Canterbury, the prior of Lanthonie, the prior of Cartmell, the abbott of Kentesham, the abbot or prior of Osney, of Bathe, and the master of St. Thomas Acres . . . which they . . . not regarding the defence, no good order of the same . . . have suffered the Kings enemies to encroach and enter into for their dominion and possession. So that now they (the King) re-enter into possession." This Parliament repealed Poyning's Act.

Their next Act was to "Authorise the King, his heirs and successors to be supreme head of the church of Ireland." This was followed by an Act forbidding appeals to Rome,— similar to the English Act—such appeals to be in future made to " the King of England and Lord of Ireland . . . whatsoever he be, of this land of Ireland, for the time being." Various " attaintments " were made, and Acts passed to prevent the interference of the "foreign head of the church"; notably an Act prohibiting "proctors" from being members of Parliament, proctors being obliged to be clergy. They "have no right, any voice or suffrage in the same, but onely to be there as counsailors and assistants to the same. . . . That the said proctors ne any of them . . . ne any member in parcel of the same Parliament, ne shall give, ne shall have any voice, opinion, assent, or agreement to any act . . . enacted in any Parliament within this land." Chapter xxiii. of this Parliament goes specially into details of the "mischief attending the Pope's authority" which did "obsueat and wrest Gods holy word and testament a long season from the spiritual and true meaning thereof, to worldly . . . craftie devises . . . inventions set forth under the cloke of virtue . . . only to promote and establish his dominion as well both upon sowles and bodies as also temporal goods of all christian people, excluding not only Christ out of his Kingdom . . . but also Kings . . . out of their dominions . . . also spoyled this (the Kings) land of Ireland, yearly of innumerable treasure . . . persuading them by lawes and bulls . . . of irronious views of the Kings laws . . ." (so that) "for the publique weal of this land (it is necessary) *to exclude that foreign pretended power . . . usurped within this land.*" After November 30th, 1537, it was illegal for the See of Rome to interfere, or to do anything "dirogatory to . . . the lawes, customs, and usages of this land." [No Church ceremonies were touched or prejudiced by this Act, neither was the Church's right of dispensation interfered with.—A. M. R.] Besides the various Acts connected with Church matters and foreign interference there were Acts for protecting fisheries and old leases; also, that parents unable to keep their children to school beyond ten years of age, should "put them to handicrafts or husbandry on pain of 6s. 8d." In the thirtieth year of the King, Parliament was called in Dublin, June 13th, before Anthony St. Leger, and visited Limerick and Trym, ending November 19th, 1512. The first Act of this Parliament was to order that "the King of England, his heirs and successors, be Kings of Ireland." Land Acts, Church Acts, Tythe Acts, freeing of those who were "compelled" to take Church vows, Acts for building churches, vicarages, and against beggars, who were "to be stript naked and whipt" as found in each parish "where they had not a license to beg." In Lymerick, in February 1512, an Adjournment Act was brought in, and fresh regulations made as to the persons to be chosen for Parliaments.

Rot. Parl., c. 16.—"That whereas the King's Irish enemies have been heretofore of great force and strength within this land of Ireland, by reason whereof they have charged divers of the King's towns and faithful subjects with tributes and exactions, for consideration that the said Irishmen, which do take the said tributes should defend the King's said subjects, which they have not done, ne do not, and yet the King's said subjects at the charge do pay them the said unlawful impositions to their utter impoverishment. . . . The King having respect to the povertie of his said subjects . . . ordained, That no manner Irish man within this land of Ireland, shall have any tribute, exaction, or other unlawful impositions of, or upon any the King's townes or faithful subjects," etc., etc.

Rot. Parl., c. 23.—Act against the authority of the Bishop of Rome.

Rot. Parl., c. 26.—The Irish habit prohibited in "this part of this his (the King's) land in Ireland, that is called the English Pale." Clause 3, "the English tongue to be taught the people." "Householders to live after the English fashion."

33 *Hen. VIII.*, 2 *Session, c. i.* (1542).—" Forasmuch as
. . . it was enacted . . . no parliament should be . . . held
. . . or proroged in any citie . . . but in Dublin or in
Drogheda, ne that no parliament be prorogued . . . over
and above two times. Neyther that no knight, citizen ne
burgesse, should be chosen in parliament, but such as dwell
within counties, cities or townes where they be chosen . . .
that such . . . spend fortie shillings in fee simple . . . and
ever proctor to be within same diocesse . . . if any be
otherwise . . . that all acts . . . made in that parliament
shall be voyde, which acts considering the distance of
borough townes and obedient shires from Dublin and
Drogheda . . . and the dangerous and perilous passage
by the way, by the occasion of the kings rebels . . .
wherefore it is enacted . . . by this present parliament
. . . the acts summoning parliament in any other city . . .
and the choosing of knights, etc. . . . within the same
diocesse . . . shall be voyd. . . . Provided . . . every . . .
knight . . . be chosen by the greater number of inhabitants
present . . . be chosen as before rehearsed . . . despend
. . . or have freehold in the counties of 40s. yearly. Every
inhabitant electing otherwise forfeit £5. . . . every
knight otherwise elected forfeit £100."

An Act for the suppression of Kilmainham and other religious houses.

33 *Hen. VIII.*, c. v.—" Whereas Sir John Rawson knight, late pryour of the pryory or hospitall of St. Johns Jerusalem . . . in this realm of Ireland, and other . . . abboths, pryors, abbesses, prioresses, and other ecclesiastical governours of diverse monasteries, etc. etc. . . . in Ireland of their owne free and voluntarie mindes . . . without constrainte . . . of any manner of person, scithens the fourth day of Februarie in the seven and twentieth reign of . . . our Sovereign Lord, by the due order and course of the

common lawes . . of Ireland, by writings . . . under their common seal . . . have severally given, granted . . . and confirmed all monasteries . . . and other religious houses . . . privilidges . . . manours lands . . . to our saide lord the King. Renouncing the same . . . said houses given to the King and his heires forever. . . . All houses hereafter dissolved with their revenues shall be vested in the King." All leases and rents of such premises to stand as settled by the King's patent. Monasteries before exempt from visitation, henceforth open to visitation.

In 1563 Meath was divided into east and west, " because it was so greate and large in circuit, and the West part thereof laid about and beset with divers of the Kings rebels, and that in several partes thereof the Kings writs for lacke of ministration of justice, have not of late been obeyed, no his Graces lawes put in execution. And that the said sheriffe of the saide shire, for the time being, most commonley hath beene one of the inhabitants of the English pale, . . . within the same county and is not able to execute the Kings processe . . . and other things belonging to his office . . . in the west . . . in consideration whereof it is wise there be two sheriffs."

This was the last Act of Henry VIII.'s Parliament.

The first important Act of Philip and Mary was an Act explaining and reviving Poyning's Act. An Act was also passed against " corserie,"—buying horses, colts, etc., intending to fatten them on " the lord's land " and then selling them " very deere." It was a hindrance to husbandry—hurtful to the wealth of the realm—as these men idled and robbed and would not work. Therefore, after " 1st May, any cottier or labourer, horseboy or kernaugh shall not buy any horse," etc., upon pain of forfeiture and fine of 40s. Those who want horses for farm work may keep them from August to October. This Parliament made an Act against making *aqua vitræ*, as thereby "grain and other things were wasted . . . to the loss of the poor ": by paying a fine and getting license therefore "some may make it for their own use only."

An Act was made repealing statutes against the See of Rome; and the Bull of Paul IV. forgiving the subjects in England and Ireland was published. Parliament confirmed the Pope's dispensation, and declared all churches, monasteries, etc., as in possession of Henry VIII. and Edward VI. to be now confirmed to her Majesty. Clause 6 of this Bill "that whoosoever shall by any processee obtein out of eny ecclesiasticall courte within this realme, or without, or by pretence of anie spirituall jurisdiction, or otherwise, contrarie to the laws of this realme, inquiet or molest eny person or persons, or bodie politique, for eny of the said manors" shall suffer as by Act made in Richard II., and shall forfeit. Clause 8 says, title of "Supreme Head" never could be justly attributed to any King; yet, that Acts having these titles "be kept and pleaded." The Pope is also reinstated in "such power" as he had before over his people in Ireland. This was immediately followed by an Act "for reviving of three old statutes made for the ponyshment of hereticks."

3 & 4 *Philip & Mary, chap.* xiii., enacts, "any person comying of Scottes, being men of warre . . . within this realm (given) eny wages, bonaghts, forreyn or other enterteynement, or hiere for the service in warre . . . for such offence . . . shall be adjudged high treason . . . and everie of them . . . convicted thereof . . . shall suffer the poynes of death, and losse . . . all goods . . . land, etc. . . . Iff any person born within . . . Ireland doo hereafter (without permission) contracte matrimonie . . . with eny Scottishe man, woman or mayden . . . they shall be adjudged felons and shall suffer poynes of death, losse of goods," etc.

This was followed by another, wherein the Queen relinquished her right to the churches, etc., vested in her, which thus lapsed to the Pope. This Parliament, fruitful of Acts for benefiting the Church, ends with one "aginst bryninge in Scotts, reteyning of them, and marrying with them." The penalty for so doing was death and forfeiture of goods and lands as of a felon.

The next Parliament met January 12th, second year of Elizabeth; dissolved February 1st, 1560. Its first Act was to restore to the Crown the *ancient jurisdiction over the State ecclesiastical and spiritual, and abolish all foreign power repugnant to the same;* to re-establish Acts of Henry VIII., and repeal some of Philip and Mary, specially that reviving the three statutes for punishing heretics: no one who would *not take oath of obedience to the Crown* to hold office.

Chapter ii., clause 1, altered the Book of Common Prayer. If people failed to attend church they were fined 12d. for the use of the poor, to be collected by the church-wardens. Various Church regulations were made, and it was ordered that churches may maintain all church ornaments as they were, unless hereafter otherwise ordered.

The next meeting of Parliament was in Dublin, in May, before Lord Sidney, and was prorogued December 12th, 1569. The first Act was claiming a subsidy; the second, making a law to regulate tanning; the third belongs to attainted lands; the fourth Act makes "the five *best* Irish in a county responsible for all those of their surname." In the third session of this Parliament Shane O'Neil was "attainder," and the name of O'Neil extinguished by law. Chapter iii. of this Parliament the Queen is entitled to the lands of Thomas Fitz Gerad, Knight of the Glanne or valley-lands in Munster, because the said Thomas and his son have been executed for committing "sundry willfull murders." People were forbidden to keep swine near the rivers, as they destroyed salmon fry; neither flax nor hides may be put, without licence, in fresh water, because so doing poisons the people. In the fourth session of this Parliament the Earl of Kildare, his brothers and sisters, were restored to their blood.

In the thirteenth year of Elizabeth manufactures of "stuffe from wooll flocks, lynen yarn, woollen yarn, sheepsfell, calfell, goatfelle, red deerfell or fallow deerefell shall onley be sold by free merchants of the towns." English merchants bringing other goods may buy these cloths from the authorised persons. In 1571 John Oge Fitz John, Knight Fitz Gybbons, was "attainder," and lands forfeited.

In the twenty-seventh year of Elizabeth, April 1st, Parliament sat before John Perrot, and had two sessions ending May 13th, 1585. In 1586 comes the "attaindor" of the late Earl of Desmond and a large company of others for high treason. And so on to the end of this reign—each Parliament more occupied in "attaindors" and securing of "the people" from depredations of the enemy than in improving the resources of the country. The making of laws and repealing of previous laws occupied Parliament, where it was complained; local jealousy, private feuds fomented by "foreign aids," were keeping the country unsettled, and giving opportunity to the Irish enemies to come in and "spoyle" settled lands.

In 1612 James I.'s Parliament passed an Act repealing Acts passed "concerning the natives of this kingdom of Ireland." Whereas in King Henry VI.'s an Act was passed not to hold "fair or market . . . amongst the Irish enemies," etc., etc., marrying Irish, or fostering therewith, all these statutes shall now cease, in hopes that by "Liberty of commerce and marriage they may grow into one nation." Acts against the Scots were also repealed. Free pardons, except for certain murders and other heinous crimes, were also given by the King.

In 1615, in the last session of Parliament, after much discussion and several dissentients, it was decided by the House, "Every Knight of a shire be allowed thirteen shillings and fourpence Irish *per diem* from the country during their attendance in Parliament, every citizen of a city being a County in itself ten shillings sterling, every Burgess six shillings and eightpence *per diem*, which was thus rated so high for divers considerations then seeming good to the House; but now, the House entering into further considerations, do think fit and so order, that, during the present Session of Parliament, and ten days before and ten days after, every Knight of the Shire be allowed but six shillings and eightpence, *English per diem*, every citizen five shillings, every Burgess three shillings and fourpence, unless special agreements were made, when those agreements hold good. The House to meet at six in the mornings."

The next Parliament met 1634, in the tenth year of Charles, when it was ordered henceforward "yeas go into the next room; those of the contrary opinion, being noes, shall stay within." A Bill for "working the materials of this kingdom of Ireland into manufacturs" was passed. Another to restrain "the converting of arable land into pasture" also passed. The Bill obliging bows and arrows to be imported by all merchants repealed. In 1635 an Act was passed preventing ploughing by the tail, and pulling the wool off living sheep.

In 1634 Parliament opened in Dublin, when, by the King's speech, the Parliament was ordered to "restrain such as have not been seven years apprenticed, nor or exercised in the trade, who, if they should be enabled to make manufactures might introduce many inconveniencies in trade . . . restrain them from making broad cloaths."

On the opening of this Parliament Mr. Serjeant Eustace

was chosen Speaker, and in a florid speech adverted to the state of the country. As this speech is, in part, apposite to the present time, a lengthy extract will be interesting:—

"The time was, and not very long since, when the Judges of our land were as it were, impaled within the English Pale, and went no further; but now their circuit is like the sun, from one end of the kingdom unto the other, and there is no place therein where their voice and sound is not heard. The Brehone law, with her two brats of Tanistry and Irish Gavel kind, the child of the bond woman, are cast out as spurious and adulterate, and every man desireth and rejoyceth, that the common law, which is the child of the free-woman, should reign over them. Let not, O God, this scepter depart from our Judah, nor such law givers from between his feet, until Shiloh come. . . . What people in the Christian world—besides ourselves and our fellow subjects—have enjoyed so long and continued peace, in these later times as we have done? . . . Good! Good! what a time was, when there was nothing heard but the ratling noise . . . the shrieks of the wounded and slain, when this island did as it were, swim in a sea of blood. . . . But these black and sad times are in a manner forgotten by reason . . . of the peace we have enjoyed; I only touch upon them, that *contraria juxta se posita clarius ducescunt*; for every one of us now doth sit in safety at home under his own roof; our swords are turned into ploughshares." After rejoicing "that the power and freedom is given unto us, that England cannot make laws at this day to bind our estates without our own consent," he goes on to "set forth our happy condition." Many walled towns, stately houses built, gardens and orchards planted, "Irish cuttings taken away, Coyne and livery abolished, every man a 'little King of his own mole hill.'" What we have is our own, and cannot be taken from us. "And tell me now, whether your Irish Harp quartered with the Arms of England . . . doth not tune melodiously, and is famous over all the world? It was wont to be a sad instrument, warbling out nothing but mournful lamentations for the dead and slain, and this was when we sat by the rivers of Babylon, and all things in confusion; but . . . now . . . they make a perfect harmony. Order . . . for the goodness of everything doth consist of order, and without order the universe would be dissolved. . . . When there was nothing but disorder what was it like unto? the ruins of a stately palace. But there are the materials (of mischief) still . . . only order is taken. . . . For . . . I do humbly beseech . . . that in the debates we shall have touching the great and weighty affairs of this Kingdom . . . we contain ourselves within bounds."

When the Speaker of the House, Serjeant Eustace, opened the Irish Parliament of 1634, he gave a most encouraging account of the state of the country. His testimony is more than corroborated by other accounts, every evidence going to prove that from 1600 to 1634, Ireland made extraordinary progress in civilisation. During those years "great" houses were built, towns were enclosed, roads and bridges made, old churches repaired, new churches built and endowed, forests cleared, fortunes made by selling the forests of Ireland under the form of "pipe-staves," the land stocked, orchards planted, so that "settlers," both English and Irish, grew to be a wealthy body. The Speaker, at the close of his address, though congratulating the House on the present position of Ireland, gives a warning that there are dangers ahead. That Serjeant Eustace had grounds for his anxiety was proved even more speedily than he appears to have anticipated; and in 1639 things seem to have got into a very serious condition. At this time it was the custom to fine those members who failed to attend the House, unless their absence was satisfactorily accounted for, and a length of absence from *any cause*, even illness, was not considered "justice" to the constituents; so that if absent for long, the seat was declared void, and a new election ordered. In 1639 absences increased, fines were each day called, and only very few men "absolved" themselves from their non-attendance. Men were too busy at home, owing to the quieting of "dissatisfactions," to attend. Finally, "dissatisfaction" took the form of "Remonstrances" to the House. There were "grievances" against the clergy, the State, the "customers," and "officials" of all kinds. The first Remonstrance, presented to the House in 1640, was against "tyrannical clerics." Bills were introduced to "repress" these, and also the other grievances complained of. But evidently the administration was not as good as the legislative enactments, for, despite Bills, robbery and jobbery continued.

Tobacco was the staple import, and a source of much wealth; bought cheap, and sold dear, it made large sums of money. But complaints were constantly made in the House "that all his Majestys poor subjects suffered thereby," whilst "Monopolists" and "robbers of the Kings Majesty" alone benefited. For the latter, evil "customers" were accountable; so the revenue laws were strengthened, while from the "Monopolists" higher duties were enforced. No law, however, relieved the "ill-paid labourer," who were "poor subjects," in the West Indies. At this period honesty and fair dealing appear to have been rare, cupidity, from the King downward, the ruling passion. Through the votes of their representatives, "the people" continually complained of extortions, and demanded *one law" for the two countries*, which were inhabited by a people "derived from a common British ancestry."

NOTES—PART III.
1635—1660.

Fair laws were passed, but the laxity of administration

continued, until grievances culminated in the rebellion of
1641. When Parliament met in the November of that year,
the "thinness" of the House speaks eloquently of the disorder in the country. So few attended, none of the ordinary
fines were called, and the House "adjourned" for a month, in
hopes of a better attendance. But things grew worse
instead of better, and there is no meeting recorded until
1647, when "The Great Council and Committee of Public
Safety" assembled. The Speaker then gave an eloquent
account of their "reduced fortunes." Commissioners were
sent to England for help. Captain Schoute accused the
House of "harbouring papists traitors"; and finally the
news came that "Commissioners had arrived from
England," when the House abruptly "adjorned" (1648)
for a year.

Then came the Cromwellian period, of which the Irish
Statute Books keep no record.

In the Parliament "sitting before Stafford," 1640, the
Petition of Remonstrance was made by the knights,
citizens, and burgesses of the House of Commons. The
following extracts give an idea of its contents. "They
humbly represent . . . that diverse complaints have been
preferred to them by sundrie persons from several parts of
this kingdom, of many grievous exactions, pressures, and
other vexatious proceedings *of some* of the clergy of this
kingdom, and their officers and ministers, against the
laity, and specially the poor sort, to the great impoverishing,
and general detriment of the whole kingdom. Which . . .
after many debates . . . it was conceived by the unanimous
votes of the House, that all of them were very great and
enormous grievances, and fit to be rectified, specially those
in the annexed Schedule mentioned . . . some being most

exorbitant and barbarous . . . ought to be quite abolished, being repugnant to law and reason. And the rest . . . to be moderated, for the relief and case of his Majesty's subjects in general, especially the poor, who are most troubled and vexed in this kind." Church grievances were then listed; *thirty, as given below*, to be *entirely abolished*. "For herse cloth, six and eight pence, though there be none at all. Parish clerk, a barrel of corn for every plough, or two quarts of rye or wheat for every acre ploughed. For every corn mill two quarts every week. In Connaught and elsewhere, six pence *per an* of every couple, by the name of ' Holy-water-clerk.' The Bishops take upon them to appoint commissioners for the subsidies, and Justices of Peace to take the office of Church Wardens upon them, under pain of excommunication. Curates and Ecclesiastical persons made commissioners, and officials, *against the Canons and his Majestys instructions*. Men summoned to appear when there is no informer, no libel, but sworn to answer unto articles. Married couples that live together, brought to Court to prove their marriage and when prove it obliged to pay seven shillings for a dismiss. The Court gives . . . two shillings *per diem* to the church wardens besides men called Inqusitors, and others that attend the Court, which is collected of the parish. If the parishoners refuse they are cited, not discharged until they pay fourteen shillings. Church wardens pay for their preferment eight shillings and six pence, some fourteen shillings, fees. In the diocess of Waterford, and other places every Church Warden must buy a book of articles of the *Register*, and pay two shillings and sixpence for it . . . worth three pence. For every certificate entered by Church Warden of the state of the Church two shillings and eight pence. When their times are up Church Wardens pay for their discharge twenty shillings. Four taill of corn, being nine sheaves (the taill, for every plow besides tythe corn in *specie*. One sheaf of all sorts of corn for every horse in the plough, called *Vmne-na-bracke*. Two and thirty quarts of oats and one quart of wheat for every garran in the plow, by the name of Lent oats in Lent time. *Quides* or *refections* of every parishoner now raised to a constant revenue. *Coshers* three times a year of each parishoner, which is one shilling for every garran in the plow, and such as have no plough but dig with spade one shilling *per an*. In Connaught a *mescan* or dish of butter, once *per an* in summer of every parishoner, worth six pence or eight pence. Every man that dies *Multue*, by the name of annointing. From a poor man, that hath but one cow, they take that for mortuary: from one that is better able his best garment for mortuary; if a woman her best garment for mortuary, and a gallon of drink for every brewing, by name Mary-gallons. For every beef killed for funeral the hide, the tallow, and do challenge a quarter besides. In Connaught, and other places, they take a *Multue*, two lambs and the best garment of the defunct, as well in the parish where he dies, as where he is buried. In Connaught, and other places, they take four pence or six pence *per an* of every parishoner, for soul money.

"For Portion Canons, the tenth part of the goods, after debts paid. A ridge of winter corn for every plow, called St. Patrick ridges. Also Rood-sheaves—a sheaf for every acre welded. For christenings two shillings and sixpence, and more, besides book money. If a beggar dies in the house, owner must pay three and six mortuaries, if a child is born ditto. If a dead body be carried through a parish on the high way only, must pay duty as if buried there." This list is followed by a list of Church fees to be allowed for marriages, births, deaths, and other Church matters, but to be *all reduced*. Schools ordered to be kept and not neglected as heretofore. Large subsidies were ordered by the House to meet His Majesty's war expenses.

A Bill brought in for providing Church and Free schools; also a Bill for the relief of the poor orphans, old, blind and impotent persons, poor and not able to work, and for punishing rogues and beggars, and setting them on work.

In this Parliament a large number of Naturalising Acts were passed, and also Bills, similar to the Church grievances, to regulate and reduce fees of "temporal courts" and *all* officers of justice.

The Knights, Citizens, and Burgesses made another Remonstrance to the Lord Deputy, through the Lord Speaker, attended by Sir Donogh MacCarty, Lord Robert Dillon, Sir Edward Fitz-Harris, Sir Hardrees Waller, Sir James Montgomery, Mr. Nicholas Barnewall, Sir W. Coll, Sir Robert Travers, Sir Charles Coote, and the Vice-Treasurer, showing—"That in all ages past, since the happy subjection of this kingdom to the imperial Crown of England it was and is a princely care . . . vast expense of treasure and blood, that their loyal and dutiful people . . . of Ireland, being now for the most part derived from British ancestors should be governed according to English law . . . this kingdom was, until of late, in a flourishing state . . . the said people gave his Majestys Royal and Princely occasions £150,000, also £120,000, £40,000, and six entire subsidies in the tenth year of his reign (other large sums follow, which they pray may not be a precedent as) this kingdom is reduced to that extreame and universal poverty that they cannot now pay two subsidies." (1) Because of the *apparent* decay of trade owing to increased "rates and impositions"; (2) unlawful fees exacted by everybody; (3) length of "civil causes"; (4) failure of carrying out the laws; (5) *estates not settled as designed by law*; (6) tobacco-cheating; (7) monopolies "to the

advantage of the few . . . impoverishment of the people;
(8) extremely cruel proceedings of Commissioners, whereby
"the worthy plantation of Londonderry is destroyed";
(9) *the ecclesiastical reliefs sought, not carried out as ordered*;
(10) "the exhorbitant and barbarous fees and pretended
customs exacted by the clergy, against the law"; (11) debts
of the King to the country "very heavy"; (12) owing to
law of 1635 preventing any to leave Ireland without a
licence from the Lord Deputy, the people have "no access
to his Sacred Majesty to declare their grievances," as they
had in ages past "since the reign of King Henry II.,"
as "great fees are exacted for every license"; (13) the
late Attorney-General acting "contrary to the laws and
privileges of the House," "subverting Parliament"; (14)
"that by the powerfulness of some Ministers of State in
this Kingdom, the Parliament in its actions hath not its
natural freedom"; lastly, "all the Gentry, Merchants, and
others of his Majestys subjects of this Kingdom, are . . .
very near to ruin and destruction, and (officials as named) . . .
very much enriched" by dishonest practices. Therefore they
request an enquiry and to have these grievances redressed.

The Parliament was adjourned November 9th, 1641,
until the 16th of the month, because the House was so thin.
As it had been ordered (at previous sitting) that "the
House Save unto itself, by protestation, the rights and
privileges of Parliament." Apparently this "adjournment" was for a much more protracted period, for the next
"Session" named is 1647, when "thanks" are given to
Captain Plunkett "That after his address, one hundred
pounds more added, and that he hath now made it one
thousand pounds; whereof sixty pound were sent to
Catherlogh in money, and he will deliver in *tobacco* to the
value of £940, at nine pence the pound, for the safe guard
of the city and relief of other garrisons." "Ten persons

undertook" £150 March 29th, £150 March 30th, and so on, for the "protection of the country; and "acknowledgements" of these sums are given by "His Excellency"—"thirty five pounds weekly, for a month . . . to the Captain and guard . . . to strengthen the guard of the Castle." It is also ordered, "the Castle gates not to be opened after nine at night, except by order of his Excellency." A fast is observed, those not "observing" to be fined, and proceeds to go "to relieve the poor." *Tobacco* sent for relief of garrison to be put into the hands of Mr. Garrat Vanhoven, Mr. Isaac Ablive, Mr. Thomas Springham, and order given "that no other tobacco be sold . . . in the English quarters until the said tobacco be sold off."

On May 7th, the Speaker (Sir Maurice Eustace) announced a member of that House was reported to be in correspondence with the rebels (Cosney Molloy). He is freed from the charge. It was ordered a committee of the House should consider the petition of "the distressed" clergy. A dispute arose as to who should take the chair (of committee); some called for Dr. Cooke, others Mr. Lewis. Captain Theodore Schoute (Messenger of the House) returned from England with the tidings, "between nine and ten hundred foot and six hundred horse with able men and money are at Chester, and that they are coming over. Sixty pounds to be given to every man that comes over." On the 26th, the Speaker announces: "the little fortune in Kildare is lost, and that was left I brought to Irishtown . . . by the gallantry of Horse . . . that Lieut. Harman may command those soldiers." Later on Baron Hilton says :—" The gate of Justice is laid up, despoiled of means . . . no protection is valid." The House by Bill declare the doings of this (an irregular) Parliament legal.

On June 9th it is announced that Commissioners are

coming out of England to the Parliament. Again the
clergy seek protection. Captain Schoute accuses the
"papists" in the Parliament. On June 18th, 1647,
this Parliament ordered that, until further orders of this
House, John Cromwell be not interfered with, after which
the House was prorogued to June 15th, 1648. On June
15th, 1648, the House met. By unanimous consent, Sir
M. Eustace took the chair as Speaker. The only business
done was, that Mr. Brereton moved they adjourn for a
year, Mr. Plunkett that they adjourn to March 27th next,
which was agreed.

On May 8th, 1660, before Sir M. Eustace, the House met.
With him were Roger Lord Orrery, and Charles Lord
Mountrath. This House passed an Act recognising
Charles II., " who deduced his title, not only from Henry II.,
but much older times." They renounced the "bloody and
traiterous parricide by King Charles I.," and recognised the
King's title to the Kingdom of Ireland since the murder
of his father. By a second Act, they (with the King's
sanction) make valid all *legal business enacted since* 1641 *by
Courts held under the stile or title of* "Custodos Libertatis
Angliæ Authoritate Parliamenti, etc., in the name of . . .
Oliver Lord Protector of the Commonwealth of England,
Scotland, Ireland, which are "as good as if made by
Parliament." Bills entered in the Protector's name to now
continue in the King's name, *excepting such as taken against
subjects for adhering to the King.* After passing four Acts,
the last of which is lost, this Session ceased. The second
Session was a short one for raising money. The third met
on March 4th, 1661, when Parliament ordered Thanksgiving
days in churches. This was followed by an Act detailing
the unnatural rebellion of October 23rd, 1641, "the murther
and destruction of many thousands . . . good and loyal
subjects" (of Protestant and Roman Catholic), *until it*

formed a "National rebellion of the Irish papists against your royal father of blessed memory, his crown and dignity, to the destruction of the English and Protestant inhabitants of Ireland, when, acting by a Council called by themselves, the Confederate Roman Catholics of Ireland did *first* assume, usurp and exercise the power of life and death." ... "By all said ways *disowning and rejecting your* Royal father, and your Majesty's undoubted right to this kingdom. ... Even while they treacherously used his and your Majesty's names in the outward form of their proceedings, seeming . . . to swear even unto that, which by the whole series of their deeds they denied, presuming to pretend his late Majesty's most Sacred Authoritie, even in their worst actions, all which they did to frighten his good protestant subjects from their loyalty, to blast his Majesty's honour." Several subjects by those rebels subdued, having been driven to it protected themselves, and invited the King to come over. Thanks for the King's letter from Breda, his declaration November 30th, and an account of their calling, as by him advised, a Parliament. Horrible massacres are recited, as done "by notorious rebels," which now "endeavour to conceal the same." Ask to have both laity and clerics "restored," Protestants and "innocent papists" to be included in the King's "settlement." The Lord Primate of Ireland, Speaker of the House of Lords, made a speech at the opening of this Session, wherein he said :—" Have we not, these many years, been walking through the wilderness without a Moses, without an Aaron? Hath not our flesh been torn with briars, and our loins whipt with scorpions? Hath not the tale of our bricks been doubled, and provision of straw exacted at our hands? . . . Have not the Parliaments of this kingdom been carried into captivity . . . our Senators become Peripatetics and Pilgrims to titulary Conventions

. . . when we have asked bread, have they not given us stones . . . the robe of Majesty before your Lordship *was the garment for which they cast lots* . . . Thy Lyons O England roareth not out of courage, but for hunger. Thy Lyons O Scotland was not rampart; the Flower-*de-luces* withered; and thy harp O Ireland, thy discomposed Harp was hung upon the willowes; but now you hear the silver strings of it touched by another David. . . . Glory be to God on High, peace—peace—peace unto men. The Church settled, peace unto men; your estates and liberties secured. . . . Must your own natural members be cut off (even) if they payd but a little sustenance to you, their Head? . . . His Majesty knew the Irish seas (feuds) run high, the steerage was not to be put in *fore-mast-mens* hands; few, when your Lordships (three Justices) enterance upon the Government durst take the helm—it was dark night—a long night, a stormy night, the wind high . . . a lee shore—not a (trustworthy) Sheriff, Justice of the Peace . . . every man did what was good or rather what was evil in his own eyes: religion mocked . . . soldiers without arms or money . . . estates of the people in secure . . . universal decay of trade. . . . The head cannot say it stands not in need of the feet. . . . The Irish have danced (with joy at returned peace)." He ends " we have got peace. . . . But the God of peace grant that we may hold the unity of the spirit in the bond of peace."

In this Parliament order was given "the vice Chancellor . . . of the College of Dublin . . . be desired . . . with all speed . . . to cause the Library formerly belonging to the late Lord Primate of Armagh, *and purchased by the army*, be brought from the Castle of Dublin where they now are, unto the College to be preserved for publick use . . . a catologue . . . both manuscripts and printed books . . . to be entered in the Journals of the House."

Again a Bill was passed to "repress Sabbath breaking," as by their wilful actions godless men do "as much as lieth in them, to bring the wrath of God upon this place."

All that "touched the honour" of the late Lord Strafford expunged the House; also those things which "touched the honour" of several high persons named.

The proposals of the House included—

I. That no one of the Irish quarters *except innocent papists* be admitted to dwell in walled towns.

II. "That in regard Priests, Jesuits and Friers, have been the constant incendiaries of rebellion in this Kingdom . . . they be secured (from doing evil)."

III. That strict enquiry be made about "the" priest who wrote, and "the one" who received the letter (concerning a surprise on the Castle).

VIII. That "papist" be purged from the army.

IRISH STATUTES, 1660.

The next Irish Parliament was called by desire of King Charles II., by letter from Breda, on May 8th, 1660. It sat before three Lord Justices, Sir Maurice Eustace (Speaker), Lord Orrery, and Lord Mountrath. Nothing is more affecting than the history of the misery this country had passed through, as is unfolded by the Act of Indemnity. The rewards, restitution, and oblivions of offences in this Act, are of a true kingly generosity; and the care taken, by the King's orders, " of all the conflicting interests which had grown up under usurped and other governments— unless where men were taken "in open rebellion after the Kings acknowledgement"—are most noble. Every one, except notorious leaders, might plead "innocency," and receive a free pardon; and "every man" was, "*as far as possible,*" to be "restored" to his own. Wherever Cromwell had given the "adventurers lands" they were "confirmed"; or, if these men were removed, they were to be "reprized" elsewhere. Those who could not be "restored," *because new interests had accrued*, were given, of "the Kings bounty," lands as near their own as possible. In righting the wronged, the King was careful not to create new grievances. The lands "forfeited" to the King in 1660, were those given by Cromwell to men for rebelling against the *law*, and the lands of those taken in open war against the King.

Because of the many records of the nation destroyed during the disturbance, all now found were ordered to be preserved in the State Record Office, Birmingham Tower We have dwelt at some length on this period, as no time of our history is more interesting. From this time the real "settling" of Ireland commenced, and from this time also grew those racial and religious "grievances" fostered amongst us at the present day.

NOTES—PART IV.
1660—1685.

On the Restoration, Charles II.'s Irish Parliaments "confirmed" by special Act, the general proceedings of the "Council" which recently sat under Oliver Cromwell. Special exception was made against Acts affecting such persons as were "regicides," proved actual murderers within a certain limited time, or specially rewarded for being "in arms" against the King, *after* the proclamation of May 1659. All Acts of attainder and confiscation against those who "stood" to the King throughout the rebellion were annulled, a general amnesty and restoration followed.

Dealing as it does with the Parliament immediately following the Commonwealth, of which Government there are no "Acts" in the Irish statutes, it is full of striking lessons of kingly mercy and constitutional justice, law and order. 17 *Car. II.*, c. 2, evidently framed to reinstate those "attainted" by Cromwell, while "restoring them was careful not to disturb *new interests* planted by the Commonwealth. This Act is largely quoted because there is scarcely a clause that is not of important significance, and instructive to those concerned for Ireland to-day. Taking it that Cromwell represented an unjust Protestant ascendency, and that this state of things had created an unbearable coercion of other subjects, and that Charles II. carried an olive branch to those other subjects, and was determined to right their wrongs; still he was careful not to create a fresh wrong while "restoring" them to their place as "good subjects." As clause 189 shows, it was the King and not the "newly planted" who had to pay for re-establishing order. Clause 221 shows the care taken that the "papists" who had caused so much trouble should not be allowed to live in "walled towns" where their presence would be dangerous to their Protestant fellow-subjects. The uncouth Irish names being changed by Act of Parliament to easier English accounts for many old landmarks being now effaced. The first Act of William's reign was to prevent ecclesiastics punishing by death, though to them was still reserved power to try and punish in lesser way those who transgressed Church rules. Act III. of 7 Wm. III. declares the Acts of James' *pretended* Parliament null and void. Other Acts follow showing why "papists" had to be restricted: *because* they stirred the people to rebel against the law, and *because* they brought subjects of the French King into the country to kill the Protestants and destroy the King's power. Act after Act of a penal nature was passed to prevent a repetition of this evil,—9 *Wm. III.*, c. 1, being at last passed to drive *all Popish ecclesiastics out of the kingdom*, because of the desolation and ruin which they caused.

These Acts of two hundred years ago speak to us to-day, and show the same agency now working amongst our people. The penalties and measures adopted then were necessary, because a foreign power, through the Stuart dynasty, were working upon the Papal power to appoint Stuart nominees in Ireland to subjugate Ireland through their clergy, and thus subvert the English and Protestant interests which, through many generations, had made us part and parcel of themselves. Such penal laws are not a necessity to-day; but history repeats itself, and it were wise to see that the efforts of "alien" powers to subvert English interests in Ireland are not allowed to overcome law and order in the land.

IRISH STATUTES, 1660—1685.

17 *Car. II.*, c 2 (1665).—An Act for Settlement of the Kingdom of Ireland. Previous Acts of William III. and Anne quoted, explained, and confirmed for the settling of the country and satisfying of adventurers. The meaning of the Act being to have " the revenues of the church settled and increased . . . dutiful and loyal subjects quieted and secured in their just possessions . . . that there may be a general . . . industry by building, planting, and all other ways of improvement, to repair and amend the desolations . . . of this kingdom." By this Act it is declared that all land and property sequestered to the King, owing to rebellion of 1641, is his without question, to be disposed of as he will. All who since 1659 were in possession and who are not now proved "innocent" persons forfeited their lands to His Majesty. Also the lands belonging unto "John Fitz Gerard, *alias* FitzGerald of Innishmore commonly called the Knight of Kerry—Captain John Magill of the County Down—Geoffry Fanning of Ballingary . . . or any of their ancestors whose heirs they are . . . or of persons in trust for them . . . upon 22 Oct. 1641 . . . are forfeited . . . and adjudged to have been . . . in the actual possession of

... your said Royal father." Lord Strafford's inquisitions declared void. All church, university, hospital, or other corporate property previously exempt, *not* now by this Act vested in the King. The King is not to take away any property vested in Protestants previous to October 22nd, 1641, unless it be proved they hold for " any Irish papist or Roman Catholic . . . not adjudged innocent." Officers given lands for service previous to May 7th, 1659, to continue therein and be confirmed in *two-thirds* of said lands. Protestants to be first provided for. Soldiers, adventurers, and Protestant *purchasers* of lands in Connaught or Clare before 1663, which lands are now restorable to original owner, to be provided for by two-thirds in other lands—" Protestants first and with all speed."

As little change of ownership as possible to be made so as to preserve improvements. The Commissioners are therefore to consider " convenience " and " continuity," and to provide suitably for the " restored " without unduly interfering with those *now* " planted " in and enjoying the lands. Soldiers and adventurers to retain possession of their lands, notwithstanding mistakes. Those removed from the Duke of Ormond's lands " reprized elsewhere." Deficient adventurers to be supplied with adjacent lands. Such soldiers and adventurers as received lands in Ireland for arrears in England and Ireland, to have claims divided, and they to be "*satisfied*" in *Ireland only for Irish arrears*. To save expense several persons may join in same letters patent, so as land does not exceed 15,000 English acres. Care to be taken of "Free School" grants. A yearly rent of £300 a year to be settled for ever upon the Provost of Trinity College. The " heirs " of certain named persons, deceased, to be provided for, and a house in Limerick set apart for the Bishop of Limerick for ever. For this house and land " in length three score and six yards, in breadth twenty and nine yards, lying at the backside thereof," running to the " highway adjoining the wall of the said city," recently rented by Edward Bishop of Limerick, at one pound per annum, to be given to William, present bishop, and his successors for ever.

Clause 36 declares no papist, or persons not taking the oaths, to be permitted to purchase houses in corporations without special licence from the Chief Governor and Council. No officer who served since 1649 can *let* or *devise* such house to any "papist or popish recusant or person" refusing to take oath of supremacy and allegiance, on pain of forfeiture of double the value of such house. To prevent the ruin and decay of corporation houses, they add £100,000 to be distributed as speedily as possible. Lord Mountrath, deceased, his heirs to have £6000 for service before 1649; Lord Conway to be satisfied for same arrears. Maritime towns to be placed in safe hands. Lord Roscommon and Lord Orrery to be satisfied of arrears " by forfeited houses in Limerick to the value of £50,000 at 8 years purchase. Debentures offered in payment by said Earls to be accepted by Treasury."

One year's rent of lands of Irish papists, as let in 1659, to be paid to the Treasury in two fragments; any twenty days after date to pay double money; other adventurers and soldiers the same (the lands settled by Erasmus Smith to any pious or charitable use only excepted).

Clause 45.—Whereas his grace the Duke of Ormond and the lady his wife are entitled to quantities of forfeited lands in Catherlagh, Galloway, Waterford, Dublin, Kildare, Meath, Cork, Kerry, Kilkenny, Tipperary, and other places, which would if now given "greatly obstruct and hinder the settlement now intended . . . the full sum of £50,000 be paid out of the money aforesaid unto his grace . . . in lieu and recompence . . . for all such."

Clause 46.—Whereas . . . houses . . . in the city of Kilkenny . . . Clonmel, Carrick, Callin, Inistioge, Traly and Dingle were held October 23rd, 1641, by the said Earl or in his wife's right, he shall now have them in place of arrears due, paying to His Majesty one shilling and sixpence yearly out of every twenty shillings yearly rent.

Estates of regicides bestowed upon the Duke of York, excepting those already apportioned to Michael Archbishop of Dublin, Lord Aungier, Sir George Lane and Sir Hercules Huncks; Lord Anglesay and Duke of Albemarle provided for, Eniscorthy and all the estates of Robert Wallop, confirmed to Lord Southampton, Ashley, and Sir Orlando Bridgeman and Sir Henry Vernon.

Sir William Penn provided with £1000 a year in Cork. Several other noblemen and others confirmed in lands held previous to 1641, and several others "particularly restored"; "if any be fraudulently restored to more than belonged to them in 1641, to forfeit double the value."

Decrees for innocent Protestants absolutely confirmed. So for innocent papists. People declared innocent and restored, but not to sue for mesne profits.

Lord Tyrconnel restored and pardoned; lands held in possession of Trinity College excepted; these lands being given by the King to the College when forfeited are to be the College property for ever. Lewis Lord Clanmalira not pardoned, his estate granted Sir Henry Bennet, now Lord Arlington. Soldiers to be removed therefrom and provided elsewhere; and Lord Aungier having £200 per annum therein shall have other land from Lord Arlington in lieu thereof.

Erasmus Smith's lands being evicted he receives lands in Louth in lieu thereof; and in Tipperary, if Sir John Stephens prove his claim, Erasmus Smith to be provided elsewhere, and to be allowed to sue for mesne profits.

William Montgomery, Florida, County Down, being innocent, restored to his estate, and to get his debentures elsewhere.

John Fitzpatrick, Castletown, Queen's County, restored in blood and in property as by 19 *James I*. A number of

Limerick men restored, and soldiers discharged in 1648 without provision, satisfied. Sir Henry Tint's lands in Cork secured to him as previously enjoyed.

Lord Netterville restored in blood and to part of his estate, other portions allotted to his relatives ; to Edward Smith and Sir Courtney Poole are secured the portions already allotted to them. One penny per acre to be levied to pay Sir William Petty, and for his " better encouragement to finish the several maps and descriptions" of such land as he has already surveyed.

The Earl of Kildare to receive "satisfaction" for claims as near to his lordship of Kildare as convenient. Sir James Shaen's claims to the earl's estate as administrator to late earl to be met by a grant of £500.

John Fitzgerald, John Magil, and Geoffry Fanning to be restored to such estate as the Governor shall think fit. Sir John Stephens to have Sir Brice Coghran's lands in Cork. Lord Inchiquin to receive £8000 for his sufferings. Then follows a list of others whose services are requited with money. Sir Charles Lloyd being " restored " to his lands in Limerick and Queen's County, Sir Richard Billings John, Lord Kingstown restored, the latter to have such of his lands as are bestowed upon Lord Fitzhardinge " made good " elsewhere ; other leased lands also, to remain as at present, and the value to be made good. The O'Briens restored in Clare, Sir Daniel, " now Lord vice-count O'Bryen of Clare," to be restored, " as on the 22nd Oct. 1641 . . . as also one stone house in the city of Limerick . . . allotted to Daniel OBryen Esqr. son and heir apparent of Connor OBryen . . . son of . . . said Lord OBryen." All tithes are excepted. Transplanted people to receive compensation " out of the forfeited lands undisposed of to the English protestants . . . after the several interests of his Majestys protestant subjects in Ireland have been fully satisfied."

James Fleming restored, Charles Farrel restored in Longford. Frances Darcy satisfied of her jointure. Lord Ranelagh's arrears before 1649 to be paid as provision for his daughters. Lands of Christopher O'Bryen, now in possession of Pierce Creagh in county Clare, to be confirmed to Pierce Creagh, other lands to be given in their lieu to Christopher O'Brien. Sir John Sherlocke, deceased, a good subject, taken and forced by the rebels for fear of his life to subscribe to their oath and association, and who did afterwards escape and fly to Dublin . . . who was judged "nocent" (guilty) by the Commissioners on account of false subscription, to be without any reprisal declared by "gracious permission" innocent, and his son and heir, Paul Sherlocke, restored to one-third of his estate. Nicholas Burke restored to the land of his father and two thousand adjoining acres. Lord Gormanstown restored, tithes excepted; and the assignments to Lord Mountrath, deceased, to be first satisfied. Richard and John Grace restored, excepting impropriations and tithes, and the houses in Kilkenny; the soldiers and adventurers in possession, to be first satisfied. Patrick Archer restored, under like conditions. Lord Clanrickard's letters patent confirmed, the time for paying £10,000 to Lord Muskerry, being extended three years, the lands to pay debts of ancestors.

Lord Mountrath's heirs and assignees to enjoy the land he was possessed of 1659, excepting those decreed to be restored, for which they are to be reprized. William Barker also to hold such lands in Limerick, on same conditions as he had at such date. Sir Henry O'Neil restored in Antrim, Lord Massareene to be reprized in other lands, and to have letters patent as other adventurers. The lands of Artain, or Tartain, to be confirmed to Sir Nicholas Armourer. Sir John Fitzgerald, in 1640, having bequeathed to King Charles I. land "then belonging, and of right appertaining to the Bishop of Cloyne, now settles these lands on

the Bishops of Cloyne for ever, retaining to the Crown the
nomination to churches in this diocese.

Lands in Tipperary to be set out to Trinity College
towards satisfaction of bequest to them by Elias Travers—
666 acres, 2 roods, 26 poles, English measure, heretofore
allotted to William Sheeres for his father's adventure of
£300, which, in pursuance of a decree of the High Court
of Chancery in England, were conveyed to said College by
bequest of Elias Travers, D.D., deceased.

Richard Earl of Arran, having purchased from Erasmus
Smith, Esq., his interest as an adventurer in the islands of
Arran (Galway), all and every interest belonging to the
former proprietors before 1641; this is now confirmed to
the Earl of Arran.

Lord Dunsany restored, tithes excepted.

The claim of Eliza Massam, widow, to one thousand
acres in Slane, allotted to her, and in her possession 1659,
to be examined. Sir Robert Forth having wrongfully
ejected her, she be reinstated and he "satisfied" elsewhere.
James Rignolds restored to Leitrim; soldiers and adventurers at Loghscurr to be "satisfied" elsewhere.

Con O'Rourke, in same county, having died without heirs,
the King succeeds.

Mary Coghlan and Lady Slane's jointures to be secured
to them.

Lord Talbot restored to Malahide; such persons as
purchased the same from Susan Bastwick to be first
satisfied out of lands forfeited and still undisposed of.

Sir G. Herbert restored in the King's County as in 1641.

Sir Henry Tichborne to be confirmed in lands set forth
to him for his disbursements to the army between 1641
and 1643. If he be dispossessed of any to be reprized.

Mabell Countess Dowager of Fingal to have so much
land as shall yield her jointure.

Samuel Avery, Alderman of London, who in his lifetime adventured £1100 on lands in Ireland, the satisfaction for which was set out for him in lands in Conello, County Limerick, having quitted his own lot, and entered upon that of Sir Charles Lloyd, another adventurer in the same barony, which lot is now restored to Sir Charles Lloyd; and whereas the said Samuel Avery agreed with the late usurpers for certain customs upon merchandise, and became indebted in the sum of £10,000 to the Exchequer of England, this debt stands excepted out of the *Act of general pardon and indemnity*, and remains vested in His Majesty, Samuel Avery's right to land in Conello lapses to His Majesty in lieu thereof. Then follow the names of fifty-four restored persons, who are to be placed in their "principal seats"; or, if they had more than one house, they may take a choice, and have two thousand acres attached thereto, if they had before that amount of land, if not, they only now get so much land as they held in 1641. None of their grants so made to encroach upon the Protestants who should be first "satisfied."

Sir Thomas Esmonde restored, excepting to the lands now in the possession of the Duke of Albemarle.

Sir Edward FitzHarris, if proved guilty of murder or other cruelties in six months after the passing of this Bill, to be incapable of benefit from the Act.

The fifty-four persons removed to replace these fifty-four who are now restored must be reprized elsewhere. All *bonâ-fide* leases now made on these restored lands to hold good. Lord Birmingham, Baron of Atthunry, excepted from these benefits.

Papists are not to have advowsons or presentations to benefices, which shall be vested in the King.

John Paine, notwithstanding his acceptance in the time of the usurpers of £100 for his subsistence, shall have full satisfaction for his arrears before 1649.

Lord Mount Alexander, an infant, having been evicted out of St. Woolstan's, now in possession of James Allen, Lands of equal value to be allotted to him.

Sir John Coke's estate in Wicklow, as bestowed 12 Car. 1., are now confirmed and restored.

Thomas Cunningham and Lewis Dick having acquired 15,555 acres in County Limerick for pretended services against the rebels in Ireland, by hindering provisions reaching the Irish and relieving the English garrisons, for which they obtained from the Treasurer of the Irish adventurers an acknowledgment that they had adventured £7000, for which they had a receipt from Committee in Grocers' Hall, London, though neither ever did service on the coast of Ireland as understood; neither did they pay money as other adventurers did; yet, by colour of this certificate, they were possessed in 1659 of these acres unduly obtained: this land be now vested in His Majesty, unless said men within two months prove they did pay this £7000.

Threepence to be levied off every profitable acre set out to Papists, to the intent that £5000 be paid to Milo Power; the residue to such Roman Catholics of this kingdom as assisted in the happy restoration of order since His Majesty's restitution.

Colonel Cary Dillon, having been dispossessed of 2604 acres of land which he possessed May 7th, 1659, for service in Ireland, he is to be reprized the whole and receive £350, one year's rent of what he lost, due for the time he is dispossessed. If necessary, a commission of enquiry to sit as to the value of the castles and houses which he had built upon the property he is dispossessed of.

The King, not satisfied at the proofs of Randal Lord Antrim's "innocency," ordered a new trial, when Lord Antrim admitted his guilt, and threw himself upon the King's mercy. He is therefore restored.

Clause 189.—For the purpose of providing for old

proprietors, "to the end that more of the ancient and former proprietors may come to be restored (His Majesty) is graciously pleased to relinquish his satisfaction of the said lapsed money (of forfeited lands), and to accept . . . thirty thousand pounds sterling . . . in lieu and recompences thereof"; this sum to be raised off lands restored to old proprietors, or "granted to Irish papists."

Chappell Izzod sold by Sir Maurice Eustace to the King.

Clause 221.—This clause repeals the King's right of restoring "innocent papists" *to their houses in corporations.*

Clause 234.—"His Majesty, taking notice of the barbarous and uncouth names by which most of the towns and places in his kingdom of Ireland are called, which hath occasioned much damage . . . to his good subjects . . . and retards the reformation of that kingdom, for remedy thereof . . . new and proper names more suitable to the English tongue may be inserted, with an *alias* for all towns, lands and places . . . by letters patent . . . which new names shall thence forth be the only names to be used."

The next Act of this reign was one for legally establishing marriages unusually solemnised during the troubles since May 1st, 1642.

17 *Car. II., c.* 6.—An Act for establishing uniformity of public worship, whereby the Church of Ireland adopted the Book of Common Prayer, according to the use of the Church of England. All persons in holy orders to use this form or forfeit £5 to the poor of the parish. All teachers of schools or clergy failing to take oath of allegiance to have their places "voided as if they were dead."

Alien and foreign reformed churches allowed.

In colleges or universities services in Latin may be used.

Printed copies of the Prayer Book to be provided for each church at the cost of parishioners, on pain of £3 a month for repairs of church so long as they remain unprovided.

17 Car. II, c. 10. An Act to prevent ecclesiastical dignitaries holding benefices in England and Ireland at the same time. Any so doing, their livings to be voided, excepting Griffith Lord Bishop of Ossory, who may hold the deanery of Bangor, in Wales, until the settlement in Ireland be established.

In the twenty fifth year of Charles II. the various corporations of walled towns in Ireland were re-arranged, the methods of electing mayors and magistrates revised.

NOTES PART V.
1685 - 1700.

JAMES II. (1685 1689).—There remains no record in the Irish Statute Book of the Parliament assembled at the order of the Roman Catholic Prelates in Ireland, and held during these years.

By an Act of William and Mary, the penal statutes passed by this "unconstitutional and rebel" Parliament were expunged from the Statutes Book. These Acts are however described and quoted in *Dr. King's History of King James' Parliament, published* 1692, from which the following items are culled to give a general idea of their scope.

Under the direction of his Viceroy Lord Tyrconnell, the Protestant School of Kilkenny, *founded and endowed by the Duke of Ormonde, was suppressed*; the schoolmaster, Dr. Hinton, driven out; the schoolhouse made a soldiers' hospital, *and a charter obtained for a Jesuit college in the town.* The foundation of Trinity College, Dublin, was dissolved, the Provost, Vice-Provost, fellows and scholars seized. The furniture, books, public library, communion plate, all belonging to the College and those private persons connected therewith, were taken. "One Dr. Moore, a popish priest, was nominated Provost, one M'Carty Library keeper, and the whole designed for this fraternitie." The collegians were allowed out on condition *no three of them met together on pain of death.* "So solicitous were they to prevent the education of Protestants under persons of the same profession, that there might be none to succeed the present clergy."*

The King seized the profits of the Archbishop of Cashel, of the Bishops of Clogher, Elphin, Clonfert, and of many inferior livings, as they fell vacant, and gave them "for the maintenance of Popish priests and bishops." All tithes payable by Roman Catholics were given to Roman Catholic priests, who could recover them by common law. The same right was denied to Protestant clergy, who could only recover from Protestants by a writ *de excommunicato capiendo*, which the Roman Catholic chancellor either refused, delayed, or charged such high cost for, that they were double the value of the tithe! The Protestant clergy, were rendered "uncapable" of enjoying the tithes of Roman Catholics, but the Roman Catholic clergy were made "capable" of enjoying Protestant tithes. No Protestant bishop might claim ecclesiastical dues from a Roman Catholic; his preferment voided by his death, cession or absence, a Popish bishop was appointed in his stead. "All men to repute, take and deem a man to be a Roman Catholic bishop or dean of any place than the King's signifying him to be so, under his privy seal and signet." Priests "came with a company of dragoons and took the tithes by force." Protestants deprived of their horses, applied to Roman Catholic neighbours, who came and ploughed their land for them upon agreement of a half, third, or fourth portion of the corn to be grown. "This was enough to entitle priests to the tithe of those lands, which they immediately seized."

As there were thus vacant one Protestant archbishopric and three bishoprics, two other archbishops and seven

* We see the same tactics in more constitutional form to-day in Ireland.—A. M. R.

bishops were attainted, so that three fourths of the clerical jurisdiction of the kingdom was in the hands of the Roman Catholics, by a law of their own making. If a clergyman became a Roman Catholic he kept his living, and was exempted from the power of his Protestant bishop by dispensation. "One Gordon, Roman Catholic Bishop of Galloway in Scotland," was appointed Chancellor of the dioceses in Dublin. The King *did not claim* ecclesiastical authority over his Roman Catholic, *but he did* over his Protestant, subjects, "to destroy their religion," and hinder their ecclesiastical discipline.* Sir Thomas Hackett, Roman Catholic Lord Mayor of Dublin in 1688, said, "There was not one Protestant brought before him for theft, and hardly one for any other immorality, whereas he was crowded with Popish criminals of all sorts." The Lord's day was profaned, businesses being done on that day looked upon as a "conquest" over a Protestant, and Protestants were enticed to join in, "as a step towards conversion."

The priests boasted they would have all our churches, and celebrate mass in Christ Church cathedral, as they were given legal right to the churches in their preferments.

February 24th, 1688, the Viceroy seized the Protestant churches in Dublin, and filled them with soldiers to receive the arms of the Protestants. On September 6th, 1689, they seized them anew. In October and November they seized most of the churches in the kingdom. Luttrel took possession of Christ Church and others in the diocese of Dublin.

The Protestants complained to King James that this was a violation of his own Act of liberty of conscience. The King replied: "They were seized during his absence at the camp, without his knowledge or consent"; nevertheless, being obliged to his Roman Catholic clergy, he must not

* To-day the State claims fees from Protestant clergy in Ireland fro. which the Roman Catholic clergy are exempt.—A. M. R.

dispossess them as "*they alledged a title to the churches they had seized.*" If the Protestants thought their title better, "they might bring their actions and endeavour to recover their possessions by law." Sir Alexander Fitton, convicted and sentenced for forgery, being converted to Roman Catholicism, was given a peerage and made Lord Chancellor of Ireland. Protestants were removed from the bench to make room for Roman Catholic judges, and the *Charters were recalled from every Protestant Corporation in Ireland.*

July 15th, 1689.—Protestants were forbidden by proclamation to go out of their parishes.

On September 13th, 1689, all the Protestants were forbidden to go to church, or assemble anywhere for Divine service.

In June 1690, Colonel Luttrell forbade any five Protestants to meet together anywhere under pain of death.

The Protestants, clergy and laity, were robbed, murdered, and assaulted generally.

The house of the Protestant bishop, Loughlinstown, was broken into and plundered.

The Bishop of Waterford's house sacked; the bishop, eighty years of age, wounded in his bed.

Many of the clergy and laity were imprisoned, and remained there until the general delivery.

By Act of Parliament, 2600 landowners forfeited their lands "for adherence to the Prince of Orange." By another Act the "personal" property, of many previously deprived of land, was taken.

It was such Acts as these that instigated the action of the six apprentice boys of Derry. Alarmed for their lives, they closed the gates of that city, as a last resource for their personal safety. That desperate action on their part became the heroic deed which turned the tide of ruin.

The defence of Derry saved the English people, and is

the foundation upon which is built the civil and religious freedom of this our great empire.

Following this is the Parliament of William and Mary, which, in their fourth year, recognises their title to the throne; and then proceeds to revive Acts passed by Charles II. for the encouraging of Protestant settlers in Ireland.

In 1695 the Parliament of William III. was opened in Dublin. The first Act of this reign was to annul the Act called *Breve de Heretico Comburendo*, which permitted ecclesiastical censure to condemn to death, as passed in England by 29 Charles II., c. 9.

IRISH STATUTES, 1695—1700.

7 *Wm. III.*, c. 3.—Declares all attainders, and all other Acts made in the late pretended Parliament, by divers persons assembled at or near Dublin, May 7th, 1689, without authority, . . . acting in concurrence with King James, be void. "That said pretended parliament . . . was not a parliament but an unlawful and rebellious assembly; and that all acts and proceedings whatsoever had, made, done or passed . . . by or in said pretended parliament, should be taken, deemed, adjudged, and declared to be null and void to all intents, constructions and purposes whatsoever. That no memorial thereof may remain amongst records of parliament . . . that all shall be publickly cancelled . . . persons who hold and do not produce them incapable of employment and to forfeit £500 to the King. And whereas . . . they did pass one or more pretended Acts, whereby in most cruel and barbarous manner they did . . . attaint of high treason the greatest part of the lords spiritual and temporal, and principal Commons of this Kingdom . . . all which are hereby declared null and void. All pretended disabilities and for-

feitures discharged as if the parties so incapacitated were expressly named and restored."

7 *Wm. III., c.* 4.—Prohibits foreign education, none to go beyond seas to be trained up in Popery. Every person so going, or sending children, if lawfully convicted by any jury of twelve, to forfeit all his or her goods. Informations to be framed and answered instantly. Persons suspected may be summoned to appear.

Clause 9 explains the "mischiefs of tolerating popish schoolmasters," forbids their teaching either in public or private, under penalty of £20 and three months in prison. It is complained that the acts 28 *Hen. VIII., c.* 15, and 12 *Eliz., c.* 1, have not had the desired effect owing to connivance at Popish Irish schools. The first of these Acts ordered an English school in every parish, while the second ordered "that a public latin free School shall be constantly maintained in each diocess." These Acts are still in force, but owing to "popish schools being connived at" are not of use.

7 *Wm. III., c.* 5.—Papists deprived of arms. Houses may be searched for them. Noblemen hiding or denying such to be fined £100, and lesser persons £30 for first offence. No maker of firearms to take a Popish apprentice. No Papist to keep a horse worth £5. On paying £5 5*s.* horses of higher value may be taken from Papists by magistrates. For concealing such horses they shall suffer imprisonment and forfeit three times the value. This is intended as a perpetual law.

7 *Wm. III., c.* 21.—For replanting the kingdom left waste by the late rebellion. For suppressing Tories, rapparees, robbers, and other heinous crimes. Offenders being harboured by Papists, inhabitants of every barony to make satisfaction for burnings, maiming of cattle, etc. The Popish inhabitants only to pay when it is proved the offender is a Papist, Protestants where it is proved to be a

Protestant, or both where both are implicated. Money to be levied as ordered by statute, 10 and 11 Car. I., c. 13. Notice of claim to be lodged in twenty four hours after offence. Twenty pounds reward to be paid to "any person who shall take and convict, or kill any Tory, rapparee or robber."

9 *Wm. III., c.* 1.—Was an act for banishing *all Papists exercising any ecclesiastical jurisdiction,* and all regulars of the Popish clergy out of this kingdom. "*Because* it was notoriously known that the late rebellions in this kingdom have been contrived, promoted, and carried on by archbishops, bishops, jesuits, and other ecclesiastical persons of the romeish clergy; and forasmuch as the public peace and safety of this kingdom is in danger, by the great number of the said archbishops, bishops, Jesuites, friers, and other regular romish clergy now residing here, and settling in paternities and societies, contrary to law, and to the impoverishing of many of his Majestys subjects in this Kingdom, *who are forced to maintain and support them,* which romish clergy do not only endeavour to withdraw his Majestys subjects from their obedience, but do daily stir up the more seditions and rebellious, to the great hazard of the ruine and desolation of this kingdom. For which reason . . . all . . . popish clergy . . . shall depart out of this Kingdom before the first of May 1698." They were to remain in places named until transported, and returning after transportation to be considered high treason. Any hiding priests, after that date, to be fined £20 for first, £30 for second, and forfeiture of lands and goods *for life* for third offence. Penalty on justices failing to carry out this law, £100 fine.

9 *Wm. III., c.* 2.—Confirms the Treaty of Limerick. Allows all the inhabitants of Limerick and garrisons at that time with Irish belonging to Clare, Limerick and Kerry, Cork and Mayo, to be free to hold such lands as they possessed

in the reign of Charles II. or since. All such estates to be discharged from Crown arrears from 1688 to date of the articles of treaty. These persons to have no new right confirmed by this Act, only to be as they were before, as if not guilty of rebellion. Those absent, and in arms abroad, if they return within eight months and take the oath of fealty, if not in arms since February 1688, to be pardoned and restored. Persons pardoned from their offences from the beginning of the late King James to 1691, if adjudged entitled to benefit by this Act. This rebellion adjudged to have begun April 10, 1689, that being the day, by the declaration of February 1688, limited to the rebels to lay down arms.

9 *Wm. III.*, c. 3.—An Act to prevent Protestants marrying Papists. Protestant women with property must obtain a certificate that the man they marry is a Protestant, or else forfeit estate to next Protestant heir. Those already married not to be held capable to being guardian to any heir to the estate. These marriages have proved "pernicious" as the issue become "reconciled to popery." Any Protestant minister or Popish priest marrying a Popish woman to any of His Majesty's soldiers to be fined £20.

9 *Wm. III.*, c. 5.—This deals with special men outlawed for their rebellion and for summoning a pretended Parliament at Dublin, May 1689. They brought many of the French King's subjects into this kingdom and destroyed several thousand Protestants. These, and others previously outlawed, not excepted by the Treaty of Limerick, shall be still considered guilty of rebellion. Those who have so died in rebellion to have their estates forfeited to the King. If any Protestant prove claim to such forfeited estate they can hold. Persons who have left the kingdom without licence since April 10, 1689, and return after October 23, 1697, without any licence, to be guilty of high treason. Before granting licence for such returns, the Lord Chan-

cellor to take recognisance for £100 that the party so returning shall during residence here pay 10s. yearly to the bishop of the diocese for a school. Then follows a long list of names of those in whose favour exceptions as to time and other matters are made.

9 *Wm. III., c.* 7.—Another Act to punish evil doers. Act 9 is to the same end.

10 *Wm. III., c.* 7.—Decides those who hold lands shall not be disturbed to put back owners now "restored." Such ancient owners are now debarred from making claims on lands "settled" by letters patent. If necessary, these claims to be satisfied out of the King's lands.

10 *Wm. III., c.* 16.—Another law to prevent the return of rebellious persons into this kingdom. And thus we come to the close of the seventeenth century.

NOTES—PART VI.
1703—1781.

The eighty years' legislation of the eighteenth century are very instructive. After the Siege of Derry there was a strong feeling against the "popish party," whose influence it was believed had caused the terrible sufferings of that time. Hence through the early years of the century penal laws against Papists were passed. But even those penal laws were not as severe as at first reading is supposed; because, even a "papist," who *took the oath of allegiance to the sovereign of this country*, was free to practise his religion, and could thus do away with his "*disability.*" So that the law was not against the religious belief of the subject, but against the *disloyalty* which subjects holding those religious views indulged in. In the early part of this century "a closer union with England" was craved, as the best way of escaping the evils of the "corrupt" practices of those in power in Ireland. The noble benevolence of private charities in schools, churches, and hospitals, aided by Parliamentary grants, are striking, as also the amount of public money expended on "nursing" Irish industries. It is a curious fact that *English porter* should undersell and ruin home-brewed *Irish ale and beer*. The revelations on these trades will be pleasant reading for the temperance party. It is remarkable that two Archbishops of Armagh should endow two public libraries. With the Georges came great strides in social legislation. The military were put on a regular footing; barracks of a suitable nature, pay and clothing provided. Manufactures were widely extended, and the first Press prosecutions undertaken. Roads were made all over the country; grand juries instituted; Church laws improved; education encouraged; labourers' claims attended to; and laws passed to enable those who let their land to secure their rent. Agrarian spirit severely legislated against. The amount of four thousand children to thirty adults in the workhouse in 1773 is curious; and, apparently, *the* Dublin workhouse was the only one then in Ireland.

The enquiry into the state of the linen trade is a revelation as to how severely Ireland suffered from the strict protective laws then in force. The reason given for linen being "the better manufacture" for Ireland, and "the woollen" the one reserved for England, is curious; it being declared that linen was better and easier made in the soft, damp climate of Ireland, while the dry, crisp atmosphere in England was conducive to a "closer cloth." The evidence goes to prove that, then as now, it was more difficult to manufacture to advantage in Ireland than in England, because of the want of specie in this country, the dearness of fuel, and difficulty of transit; the indolent nature of the people, who prefer "Coshering" to work, is also mentioned.

From George III.'s accession the "popish penalties" were being continually "eased," and this very possibly "lead up" to the rebellion of '98. It is worthy of note the large emigration from Ireland to America at the close of this century comparatively speaking, almost as severe a strain on the population as it has been at the corresponding period of this century.

IRISH STATUTES, 1703—1781.

Tuesday, September 1st, 1703, began at Dublin Queen Anne's first Parliament: Allan Broderick, Speaker. In addressing the Lord-Lieutenant and House, the Speaker hopes that, "with your assistance, Ireland may in some way recover the languishing condition it is now in." The first proceeding of this Parliament was ordering a book, written by John Argil, member of this House, to be burned before the gate of the House by the common hangman, because it contained several "heretical and blasphemous doctrines and positions, contrary to the Christian religion, and the Established doctrine of the Church of Ireland"; and that he be expelled the House. The name of this book is not mentioned. On the same day a motion made that a book printed in Dublin "intituled the Report of the Commissioners appointed to enquire into the Irish forfeitures," contains in the seventy-eighth paragraph several false and scandalous assertions and reflections on the Protestant freeholders of this kingdom, and the said paragraphs being read:—

"Resolved, *nemine contradicente*, that all the Protestant freeholders of the kingdom have been falsely misrepresented . . . as persons that through length of time, and contracting new friendships with the Irish, or interpurchasing with one another, but chiefly through a general dislike of the disposition of the forfeitures, are scarce willing to find any persons guilty of the late rebellion, even upon full evidence. And that such misrepresentation hath been one of the great causes of the misery of this kingdom." John Trenchard, James Hamilton of Tullamore, and Henry Langford found to be authors of the book, and found guilty of endeavouring to create a jealousy between the people of England and the Protestants of Ireland. Bills against "Archbishops . . . and other regulars of the Popish clergy." Bills against "Tories, robbers, and rapperees" were passed. The House passed a Bill for the protection and reviving of trade; orders were also given that "all members to wear and purchase Irish manufacture." All imported goods to be highly taxed; "plain calico" taxed 1s. 6d. a yard!

Leave given for the Hollow Sword-blades Company to "take conveyances of landes in Ireland."

Owing to "decay of trade . . . the kingdom exhausted of coin . . . whereby a great number of protestant families are necessitated to remove out of this kingdom, as well into Scotland as into the dominions of foreign princes and states. That the constitution of this kingdom hath been of late greatly shaken, the lives, liberties and estates of the subjects thereof being tried and called in question in a manner wholly unknown to our ancestors. That the above mentioned mischiefes . . . have been occasioned by . . . ill meaning men, in order to create misunderstandings between England and Ireland and to get beneficial employment for themselves . . . that . . . subjects in this kingdom may be relieved from the calamities they now lie under, by a full enjoyment of this constitution, or a more firm or strict Union with England."

A list of State pensioners brought in. Of those who live *out* of the kingdom, George Rodney Bridges (put on April 30th, 1697) has far the largest sum, namely, £1600 per annum. Of those *in* the kingdom, Lord Galway and Francis Roberts have £1000 each. The Presbyterian Ministers have £1200 per annum; *two* of them, Mr. Mac-

Beckan and Mr. MacBride, refuse to take the oath, and ought to be struck off. [This whole allowance was stopped.—A. M. R.] *French pensioners in* the kingdom, £19,008; *out of the kingdom*, £5932, which ought to be struck off. Lady Dorchester, per annum, upon particular lands £5000, " in discharge of a debt she had upon the excise in England." In a petition to the Queen the "corruption" of civil officers in Ireland, is much complained of; this "corruption" is given as a reason for desiring a closer Union with England.

A Law was passed "to prevent papist parents from disinheriting protestant children, or preventing them from becoming protestants *if they so will*." Papists prohibited voting for members of Parliament, because they abused their privilege and " made mischiefes "— " *unless* they first took oath of allegiance " . . . " Which said certificate being produced to the High Sheriff . . . *they shall be permitted to vote as amply and fully as any Protestant*."

A Bill for " setting and preserving a public library forever, in a house for that purpose built by his Grace Narcissus now Lord Archbishop of Armagh . . . on part . . . of the Archbishop of Dublin's palace, near to the city of Dublin. In 1709 the Commons declare— " *We have found by dear bought experience that the Protestant Religion and British Interests in this kingdom are no longer safe, than while it is not in the power of Papists to distress or destroy them.*"

June 28th, 1709, presented a petition regarding Chichester House, in use as a Parliament House . . . which was in the twenty-fifth year of King Charles II. leased from Sir Henry Ford for ninety-nine years, at a rent of £22 for the first six months, and for the next two years and six months the yearly rent of £105, and for the residue of the term £180 . . . that now £580 be expended to make it weather tight. It is very ruinous . . . will stand but a few years.

In the year 1710 £24,000 appointed to be paid in

support of poor Palatines. . . . Three hundred more families sent out of Great Britain into Ireland, for which a grant of £9000 was made.

On the opening of Parliament, July 1711, the Commons return thanks for the lessened taxation of the country, and promise funds for repairing the damages of the "losses sustained by the late calamitous fire." Steps taken "for preventing the mischief, both public and private, which may arise by the loss of the records consumed in the said fire."

In 1713 the Second Parliament of Queen Anne was elected, and many complaints were therein made of the factious manner of the Papist and *irregular* way in which they influenced the election of members. This Parliament was dissolved by the death of the Queen, August 1st, 1714.

In the year 1725 (George I.) fishery laws were amended; the Liffey made navigable; working of mines encouraged; hemp and linen manufacturers aided; a Linen hall ordered to be built; also a chapel in Dublin "convenient for the soldiers."

It was therein complained that within the last few years Popery had greatly increased, because of "the many ways found out and practised by the Papists to evade the several laws already made to prevent the further growth of popery." It was decided by a Committee of the House "that the recommending of persons converted from the popish religion, by which they may be put too early into the commission of the peace, is highly prejudicial to the protestant interest of the kingdom," also . . . "prejudicial that any having a popish wife should bear any office or employment under his Majesty. . . ." No person to get employment under His Majesty that does not breed up his children to fourteen years of age to be of the Church of Ireland as by law established. No one for seven years after his conversion to be allowed to practise as barrister, attorney or solicitor, and unless he bring a certificate of having received the sacrament thrice every year during the said term.

ORDERS TO SECURE GREATER FREEDOM OF ELECTIONS.

In 1725 we have notice of Mr. Gwyn Needham and Mr. Richard Dickson being called before the House and reprimanded, for "having taken upon them to reprint the votes of the House in their newspaper '*The Dublin Intelligencer*,' misrepresenting the sense and proceedings of the House.

"Resolved, that the electing of persons to be members of this House, who are newly converted from the Popish to the Protestant religion, or who are married to Popish wives, or bred up, or suffer any of their children to be educated in the Popish religion is highly prejudicial to the Protestant interest in this country": not to be elected unless after seven years' conversion. "No one, who has been converted, and whose wife or children still continue in the Popish religion, to be admitted into any office, employment or place of trust in the kingdom."

The House supplicates the Sovereign, because of the "fatal consequences" likely to ensue, not to reverse "the outlawries of any of the persons attainted of treason, for the rebellions of 1641 or 1688 . . . as the Papists of this kingdom were almost universally engaged in those rebellions, and as their avowed design was to shake off the authority of the Crown of England, and to extirpate the Protestant religion, we cannot but apprehend, that the reversal of any of their outlawries must encourage new attempts against our sacred and civil rights . . . and an inlet to their professed enemies to deprive them of their fortunes. . . . We are continually alarmed by the new and restless attempts of those our enemies. . . . Their least encouragement would strike the greatest terror into all your faithful Protestant subjects in this kingdom . . . and make them apprehend their properties, *purchased* under the sanction of several Acts of Parliament, insecure against those who think it no injustice to contrive and set up pretended settlements to defeat the titles of Protestants."

In this year a Bill was brought in to improve the approach to the House for coaches and chairs. Bills to improve the roadways throughout the Kingdom, to secure the Erasmus Smith and Bishop Foye endowments, and to further free Protestant schools throughout the Kingdom. In 1727 Bills to give more power to the King regarding Church property which vested in the Crown; all Church property lapsing in Queen Anne's day being vested in the Sovereign.

In this year what may be called the first Bill to regulate labour was passed. In 1728 the order was given to build a new Parliament House on the old site. In 1729 laws regarding the tilling of the land, the relief of the poor, and better pay of the labourer were made, and thanks for good harvest publickly given by the Parliament. Also a Bill to prevent unlawful combination of workmen in their several trades against their employers. An enquiry as to the treatment of prisoners at Newgate and Blacklog prison; the prison keepers punished for undue severity.

In this year Mr. Richard Dickson again punished for publishing in his newspaper parliamentary intelligence without permission of the House. In 1751 permission given for an Hospital to be built in the Church premises of St. Mary Shandon, Cork.

In 1755 a Law to prevent tenants combining against paying the rents to the landlord, setting fire to houses or crops, or sending threatening letters.

An Act to allow Dissenters, who were not Popish, to hold commission in the militia or army.

So on to the close of George II.'s reign penal laws against Popery are continually passed, and efforts of all sorts made to "prevent the growth of Popery." The reigns of the Georges are also prolific in measures for developing the resources of the country, and putting government on what we may call a constitutional and civilised footing. In the year 1773 (George III.) there is an interesting report presented to the House of the Workhouse and Foundling Hospital of Dublin. The Workhouse had been started by Queen Anne, and in 1773 contains 1000 children above six and under twelve years of age; "old persons and children over twelve who have infirmities rendering them unfit for public service, 30; children under six, 3000; so that there needs to be servants and nurses 100." All children above six instructed in reading and writing, the Protestant religion, and several kinds of work; this work disposed of during two years has brought £785 13s. 6¾d., exclusive of the value of material and implements, and there are on hands lace and other work value £136. "This house is of great national importance, strengthening the Protestant interest amongst the lower ranks of the people in this Kingdom." There are now over 4000 children kept at a rate of £3 1s. 5d. each child per annum, and that they owe to nurses and food contractors £14,559.

This Parliament also petitions the King, on behalf of "The Incorporated Society in Dublin, for promoting English Protestant Schools in Ireland," which was started 1733, and which has by subscription, benefactions and Parliamentary aid erected several schools in different parts of the kingdom. They had a Nursery and Infirmary in York Street, now moved to Miltown Road, "a resting place for such children as are sent from the country to be apprenticed, or transplanted into parts remote from their Popish Relations." These are all taught such works as will make them useful citizens; to read and write, and the Protestant religion. Owing to the increased price of all commodities the expenses of these schools are greatly increased; so they are now reduced from 75 to 50 in number, and the yearly expenditure is over £16,000.

In 1773 there was also a Committee of the House to take into consideration "Brewing interests." It was shown that the trade was decaying, that the whole duty upon Beer and Ale does not amount to the expenses of collecting the same. But that imports have increased to 58,679 Barrels. Mr. Thwaites, Master Brewer in Dublin, has been thirty-four years in the trade, which was the most lucrative in the city. There were seventy breweries within his memory, now there are only thirty in the city. No brewer has made fair profit the last ten years. Half of them would retire if they could get sale for their utensils and collect in their debts. The increased price of malts and hops, fire, and labour has created the decay. They cannot raise the price, now make worse stuff, so the "liquor is less agreeable and nourishing for the people," who in consequence use "Spirituous Liquors," which is a "total depravation of the manners of the lower class." He remembers the journeymen of Dublin "a sober, industrious, thriving people . . . at present they are the most enfeebled, wretched set of creatures . . . almost always intoxicated with Dram drinking." *Porter* is imported from England to the loss of the Beer and Ale brewing of this country. The encouragement and cheaper rate of producing in England is so tempting, Dublin brewers think of moving to Holyhead and Carnarvon.

In George II.'s reign the "Dublin Society" was started for promoting "husbandry and other useful arts in Ireland." And they have, as now reported to the House, assisted by private benefactions, reclaimed "boggey and mountain parts of the kingdom." A Bill to oblige those who bring milk to Dublin to use "pack saddles" for transporting it, and *not* to take it on "low back cars." The Grand Jury's powers over their counties arranged; power given them over roads; to appoint County Treasurer, to oblige him to give security, and to appoint his salary.

Fisheries encouraged. Taxes for the King's Majesty increased. In Antrim, Down, Armagh, Londonderry and Tyrone, "evil disposed" persons stir up the people against the taxes, etc. A Bill to bring these "evil disposed" persons to justice passed December 24th, 1773.

The Speaker complains of the difficulty of getting the Supplies for Government in "a Kingdom so destitute of resources as this is."

In 1774 the Mayor and Corporation of Tipperary, deriving from Elizabeth, ask that Parliament aid them in defending their rights. Papists being there admitted into the Corporation "on condition of good behaviour, and on their paying a small sum quarterly, not exceeding three shillings, not less than six pence . . . which contribution these Quarter Brothers did from time to time pay . . . for upwards of ninety years past by the name of Quarterage . . . whereby they have relieved the necessities of their reduced bretheren, bury their dead, relieve their sick. Within the last few years . . . those deluded insurgents called White Boys have intruded themselves on this county, sundry of these Quarter Brothers, countenanced by those Miscreants, under the pretence of redressing grievances have refused to pay said Quarterage, alledging under some Colour of Right, that such demand is not warranted by law . . . they give every vexatious opposition that art, malice, or ingenuity could devise, to the great disquiet of the peace and good harmony of the said town."

A great enquiry into the linen and other trade usages in Ireland. Linen being advised since 1698 to be the manufacture most suited to Ireland, and woollen the better suited for England, the latter to be discouraged in Ireland, so that *except to England*, the *prohibition* duty on woollen material is high, so that "several thousand manufacturers . . . left this kingdom for want of employment . . . South and West of Ireland thereby entirely depopulated, So that yet, though at the distance of more than 70 years . . . they have not recovered a reasonable number of inhabitants," so that on November 3rd, 1703, the people did petition Queen Anne to consider "the distressed condition of the subjects in this Kingdom." During these seventy years, Parliament gave £500,000 to enlarge the linen trade in Ireland. But for this allowance of £500,000, Ireland relinquished to England the woollen trade, which had been hitherto her staple manufacture. The increase in the wearing of muslins hurts the linen manufacturer, "and always will, while they are permitted here, for they wear better than our linens." "Numbers, amounting to 10,000 in two years, of linen weavers, have gone to America, and taken their trade with them." Only one-third of our weavers now employed. Longford for twenty years employed two thousand looms, has not twenty now at work. The reasons of the decay are the high price of flax seed —£80,000 to £90,000 worth imported annually; flax farming being, owing to increase of rent, unsuitable to Ireland. We are ruined by the growth of linen manufactures in America and Great Britain, the scarcity of specie in Ireland, and from the way in which we make up our linens.

The English bounty on plain linens . . . are certainly an advantage . . . for the Irish merchants . . . are not rich enough to carry on an export trade themselves. As trade now is, "unless prevented for the future, must necessarily end in the Bankruptcy of this Kingdom." In three years, 1090 looms out of work in Lurgan; Ulster has lost 30,000 inhabitants; one-half the looms idle. In

Coleraine, one third the people gone to America. From Belfast 3511 peop'e gone to America; "the poor are in the greatest distress, the more wealthy with difficulty support their credit." The money gone with the emigrants to America. One-fourth of the looms in Dungannon idle. No public credit at home or abroad; no money in the country. In Galway 814 looms out of 1000 idle; 1000 families "gone beyond seas." In Tullamore one-fourth idle; in Clare one half, Athlone two-thirds, Moat one-third, Kilbeggan two thirds. This exodus has "impoverished the country, lowered the value of land, caused scarcity of money; too many gone to America, yet others would go, but they are restrained by poverty."

In 1778 an Act for the relief of Popish subjects passed, owing to their "uniform peaceful behaviour for a long series of years." From 1770 to 1781 several of the Acts passed in previous years to "prevent the growth of popery," were repealed, owing to the "peaceful behaviour" of the Popish party.

NOTES—PART VII.
1781—1800.

Grattan's Parliament is the next epoch. In this Parliament, composed entirely of Protestants, the first great Acts securing the greater freedom of their Roman Catholic fellow subjects, were passed. Poyning's Act was repealed, leaving Irishmen free to initiate remedial measures for Ireland. The result of this greater freedom was sheaves of Acts for improving the manufactures of the country by Parliamentary subsidies, which heavily overburthened the already oppressed taxpayers. Coercion Act after Coercion Act was inaugurated, then repealed. French aid was sought by the disaffected, and twice a foreign power came to their assistance. For eighteen years this Irish Parliament made stupendous efforts to "improve" this country's trade, to reduce the many internal jealousies, to regulate Irish affairs for the benefit of the Irish people. But all in vain. Outside influences were too many even for the energy and patriotism of Grattan, so the "agitations" of the enemies of England, working upon Irish enthusiasts, produced the rebellion of 1798. There are private journals of that day extant, giving the personal experiences of some of those who "suffered," with long lists of those who lost their lives and properties. This insurrection was short, sharp, and the quelling thereof decisive. The Roman Catholic arch bishops and bishops, with the larger part of their clergy, the Roman Catholic laity, under the lead of Lord Fingall, petitioned for "the Union," as the one hope for quelling the internal strifes in Ireland, and securing to them and their co-religionists a similar freedom to that enjoyed by those of their faith in England. In the "laws for supressing the evil disposed" of the last century, we see the almost identical measures—considerably modified in the severity of their penalties, to suit the humanitarianism of the nineteenth century—adopted by the late Unionist Government when drafting the Crimes Act.

Those who now complain of Ireland being behind the times as to postal arrangements, will be amused to learn the Dublin General Post Office is only just one hundred years in existence, and that three miles and a half an hour was the utmost speed of our posts at the close of the last century.

The dastard crimes and brutal cruelties of our modern moonlighters, are adoptions of last century methods of persuasion.

Then, as now, Government hoped, by developing the natural resources of the country, to "pacify" the people. The Act 25 *Geo. III.*, c. 60, which devotes £20,000, public money, as well a similar sum levied off Lord Conyngham's property, for the "fishings" in his neighbourhood, is but one of the many efforts made to encourage our people to work out their own industrial salvation.

The sum of money which was borrowed from England for the exigencies of Ireland, and the enormous amount of troops required in the country for the preservation of the lives of the inhabitants before the Union, are a revelation which should be studied by all now interested in the welfare of Ireland.

In this portion of the Irish Statutes we come to the close of "Grattan's Parliament." Grattan's Parliament is supposed to be the model upon which Irish Home Rulers desire to model a Home Rule Parliament, with this difference: that, instead of a Protestant Parliament they are to have one in which, if not entirely Roman Catholic, there would certainly be a powerful Roman Catholic ascendency. From the time of Richard II., stringent laws *against* the Papistical ecclesiastical ascendency in Ireland have been continually made, *because* such ascendency was "alien" and interfered with the peace of the country, subverting the people from their obedience to their lawful King. These early laws—which are the most severe in all the statutes against this "alien" Papistical power—were made by an Irish Parliament which was exclusively "Papistical," long before we had *any Protestants* in the land, therefore they cannot be classed as laws instituted by Protestant bigotry. and it is well to note that until Grattan's time the Roman Catholic Church in Ireland is called in all Acts an "alien" Church.

It is also worthy of note that all the earlier Irish Statutes refer directly to "English rebels and the Irish enemies" in Ireland. Therefore these Irish Statutes prove that no special laws were made by "the English" against "the Irish"; but that laws were made for the protection of the "settled" people in Ireland—some Irish being "settled" with the English—from the depredations of the lawless English and Irish in the land. Therefore it is apparent no "racial" hate was accentuated in those early days. Putting it broadly, from first to last the fight in Ireland has been between the law-abiding, steady people, anxious to improve the country and their own position, and those lawless persons who prefer fighting to work, who, anxious of success, desire to degrade those who are better than themselves to their own level, and who endeavour with the aid of "aliens" to take by force of "the strong hand" from the "settled people" such good things as their greed desires.

There were five hundred years of Parliaments in Ireland. Grattan's Parliament was the climax of that five hundred years of disputes as to whether order or disorder was to continue. Grattan's Parliament decided that "the Union" alone could preserve this country from anarchy and ruin, and establish securely the civilising power of our great English-speaking nationalities.

The Roman Catholic archbishops, bishops, clergy, and laity *were then almost all* in favour of this Union. They thought *then*, as many of the more educated amongst them think *now*, that "the Catholic religion is better safeguarded under the protection of the Imperial Parliament than it would be under any form of Home Rule Government which Mr. Gladstone can devise." *This* was publicly stated by Lord Fingal at the Unionist Convention in Dublin last summer. Lord Fingal's ancestor headed the list of those of the Roman Catholic laity who signed the requisition for the Union of 1800; therefore it was a strong confirmation of that requisition's wisdom, that Lord Fingal should have presided at "the Unionist" meeting of 1892, and protest as he did against any retrograde legislation, any separation of Irish interests from the Empire, any paltry Irish Home Rule Parliament being forced upon us. His closing words were, "they"—Irish Roman Catholics as well as Protestants "are devoted to their Queen, and proud to remain as Irishmen an integral and *governing portion* of the British Empire. So long as our birthright is being offered for sale to an English party, and the Empire which has risen by union is being hurried along on a downward course, we give notice to all who would tamper with our freedom, our fortunes, our lives, that Ireland will continue to block the way."

At the time of the Union, as is shown by these Statutes, care was taken to " compensate " all who " suffered " by the change. This compensation came, not by taking from one class to give to the other, but, from the National Exchequer—from the Speaker of the House to the humble doorkeeper, those who "lost their situations" were pensioned. Those who had benefited by "borough seats," extinguished at the Union, also received compensation for that loss; this compensation being given indiscriminately to those who voted for or against that Union, in place of the "patronage" of which the Union deprived them.

Whatsoever "iniquities" Ireland endured during those five hundred years were only similar to those endured by other nations while in a crude state of civilisation. Side by side, but still a little behind other nations, Ireland has progressed from barbarism to a Christian civilisation.

In 1800 we had four and a half millions of people in Ireland; we had a bitter racial and religious fight suppressed by "the strong hand," and the whole country on the brink of bankruptcy.

In 1892 our population is almost identically the same as in 1800; as a nation, we are, comparatively speaking, in a flourishing and *not* a bankrupt position.

In 1800 we had few roads in the country, vast tracts of land being therefore inaccessible; now we have railways everywhere. In 1800 our "post boy" was obliged by law to travel at three and a half miles an hour; and "hanged without benefit of clergy" if he neglected his duty. *Now*, we scoff at mails travelling *only* thirty miles in the hour, and clamour for a faster method of transmission.

Then it was hard to get "facts" before the Parliament in London, without great loss of time and money. *Now* a penny letter in twenty hours, or a telegram in half an hour, puts those in Parliament in "touch" with "the people" in every corner of Ireland.

We are now part of a great and wealthy Empire—a strong right hand, even though we occasionally have cut fingers—and we decline to be cut off and thrown back into poverty, confusion, and insignificance which would leave us a prey to the envy, jealousy, hatred, and malice of "alien" people, be they Romish ecclesiastics, French Republicans, or American-Irish.

IRISH STATUTES, 1781—1800.

21 *Geo. III.*, *c.* 11.—"An Act for the better securing the liberty of the Subject." By this Act persons imprisoned during vacation could apply to the Lord Chancellor, who "may take securities for and discharge the prisoner until next assizes." *But* "whereas persons charged with petty treason, felony, murder or accession thereto, are arrested upon suspicion only, whereupon they are bailable or not according to circumstances. . . . *therefore* be it enacted . . . persons so committed . . . shall not be removed or baild by virtue of this act. . . . The Chief Governor or Governors and privy Council may suspend this Act by proclamation under the great Seal of this kingdom, during actual invasion or rebellion, and no person concerned in such invasion or rebellion shall be bailable."

21 Geo. III., c. 16. Established the Bank of Ireland.

21 Geo. III., c. 24.—Permits Popish priests to take the oath of allegiance, and repeals penal Acts revived 9 Will. III., c. 1, and several revived by Queen Anne and previous ones of this reign. This Act does not apply to any person perverted from the Protestant religion, or interfering with members of the Protestant religion.

21 Geo. III., c. 51. "Whereas by an act passed in the eleventh and twelfth years of his Majesty's reign, intituled, 'An act for the remitting of prisoners, with their indictments, by the justices of his Majestys Court of Kings Bench to the places where the crimes were committed, it is recited, "that persons indicted for high treason may remove as well their bodies as their indictments into the court of King's bench, if that Court shall think fit, and cannot by order law of law be remitted or sent down to the justices of gaol delivery, or of the peace, or other justices or commissioners to proceed upon them; and it is therefore and thereby enacted, that in every such case, the justices of the King's bench shall have full authority and power to remand and send down, as well the bodies of all such persons as their indictments, into the counties where such high treasons or felony are or shall be charged in said indictments to be committed or done, and all other justices and commissioners of Oyer and Terminer, and every of them, to proceed and determine upon all the aforesaid bodies and indictments so removed after the Course of the Common law, in such manner as the said justices of gaol delivery, justices of the peace, and other commissioners, or any of them might or should have done if the said prisoners or indictments had never been brought into said King's bench; and whereas the said act does not extend to cases where the body of persons indicted for high treason or felony as aforesaid . . . therefore be it enacted by the Kings

most excellent Majesty, by and with the advice and consent of the lords spiritual and temporal, and Commons in this present Parliament assembled, and by the authority of the same, ... the bodies of all such persons ... where such high treason and felony are or shall be charged to be committed or done ... are removed, either by defendant, or at suit of the Crown, to command all justices of gaol delivery ... to proceed and determine upon all the aforesaid bodies and indictments so removed, in such manner as the same justices of gaol delivery, justices of the peace and other Commissioners, or any of them might or should have done, if the said prisoners or indictments had never been brought into the said Kings bench."'"

In 1781-82 for the purpose of more fully providing for the liberty of the people an Act was also passed.

21 *Geo. III.*, c. 62.—Repealing penal laws against Popish education. Schoolmasters of the Popish Church, having taken the oath of allegiance, were at liberty to teach the children of Popish parents. They were, however, prohibited taking either Protestant children or teachers; were not permitted to build or endow their school; and were obliged to obtain permission to teach from "the ordinary" of the diocese, such "permission" being granted or recalled at will of the said "ordinary." *No Papist ecclesiastic* might have such *permission*; but all laymen who took oath could take full charge of the children of Papists. Protestant schools were prohibited from taking in any Popish ushers or under-teachers.

In 1783-84, a Bill for establishing the Bank of Ireland was passed. Section 12 of this Act authorised Government lotteries for the purpose of raising £300,000 for the necessities of Ireland.

23 *Geo. III.*, c. 17, is interesting as it ordered a convenient place in Dublin should be selected for the establishment

of a General Post Office, with branch offices throughout the kingdom, "from whence . . . may be sent . . . received and dispatched." Letters *during the Session* signed by a member to pass free. Newspapers posted before ten o'clock at night to travel free. Post to travel at the rate of three and a half Irish miles an hour. In this same year another Act, obliging hawkers and pedlars to take out licences, was passed, the moneys paid for such licences to be given to the "Incorporated Society in Dublin for the promotion of English Protestant Schools in Ireland."

23 & 24 *Geo. III.*, c. 20.—" An Act for punishing such persons as shall by violence obstruct the freedom of the Corn Markets and the Corn trade; or shall be guilty of other offences therein mentioned, and for making satisfaction to the parties injured."

" Whereas every attempt to obstruct by violence the freedom of export . . . and the free passage . . . either by land or water, is not only a daring violation of the law, but must injure agriculture, and be in the end productive of dearth and famine; be it enacted . . . any person unlawfully, riotously and tumultuously assembled together, shall at any time after the passing of this act wilfully . . . pull down, demolish, set fire to, or destroy any store house, mill, granary, corn stack or other place . . . spoil . . . carry away . . . obstruct or prevent . . . seize, detain, take . . . with intent to prevent . . . the owner, driver or conductor thereof . . . shall . . . *suffer death as in the case of felony, without benefit of clergy.* Clause 2. . . . That all damage which shall be sustained by means of any of the offences aforesaid, or by any violence . . . shall be recovered . . . by the person or persons injured . . . levied as hereinafter directed (clause 3) . . . by writ . . . within six days after the receipt thereof . . . landowners and inhabitants shall make applotments (of amount) and choose such collector . . . and he is authorized . . . to levy the said sum . . . together with . . . one shilling in the pound for the sheriff's fee, and . . . one shilling in the pound for his own trouble in collecting . . . by distress and sale of the goods of every person refusing to pay . . ." (clause 4) if no person appointed to collect "within 30 days the said sheriff levy same. . . . (Clause 7) For the better preservation of the peace . . . any person riotous . . . setting fire to . . . shall be adjudged a felon, without benefit of clergy . . . and suffer death." (Clause 8) Same punishment for other unlawful persons. (Clause 10) "Actions shall and may be brought at the choice of the plaintiff in any adjoining county." (Clause 12) Money for these prosecutions to be levied off the county by the Grand Jury.

23 & 24 *Geo. III.*, c. 28.—This Act is to "secure the Liberty of the Press, by preventing the Abuse arising from the publication of traiterous, seditious, false and slanderous libels by persons unknown." Penalties, heavy fines.

23 *Geo. III.*, c. 30, of this year deals with Justices of the Peace. No one could obtain the Commission of the Peace who had not a "freehold estate," or some "great estate" of £300 yearly free of all encumbrance. This Act to be in force from September 29th, 1784, for twenty-one years, "and to the end of the then next Session of Parliament."

At this time it was illegal to have a "glass house," that is, manufacturing of glass, within a certain distance of Dublin. Nevertheless there was "a glass house in Mary's Lane," which it was proposed to remove for improving the town; so the "Commissioners" were authorised by Parliament to pay any sum under £400 to the proprietors on pulling it down.

23 *Geo. III.*, c. 33, appoints £15,000 to be paid in bounties to encourage the following manufactures—wool, cotton, thread, iron or copper. Those appointed to this

Commission were the Duke of Leinster, Hon. John Foster, Right Hon. Luke Gardiner, Sir Lucius O'Brien, Sir John Parnell, Samuel Hayes, Travers Hartley, David La Touche, Alderman Warren, etc. Any seven of them might direct, limit, or appoint the awards.

This was followed by an Act ordering the destruction of all "glass-houses" in or near Dublin "without compensation," as they were injurious to the public health.

At this period it is apparent care was taken not to give undue votes to Protestant party, as when the "settlements" of "Geneva and other foreigners" were naturalised, special oath was taken, that they should neither vote for, nor be elected as, members of Parliament.

23 & 24 *Geo. III.*, c. 34.—"An Act for the relief of prisoners charged with Felony, etc." Persons in custody on suspicion thereof, as accessories thereto, though no bills of indictment are found against them, *or they be acquitted on their trial* . . . *nevertheless* they are frequently detained for certain fees . . . be it enacted . . . that prisoners who now are, or hereafter shall be charged with any crime or offence whatsoever . . . who . . . *shall be acquitted* . . . shall be enlarged without any fees." This Act repeats several stringent measures adopted towards prisoners generally.

23 & 24 *Geo. III.*, c. 38.—" Further provides for the peace of the country." All strangers settling in the country to take a stringent oath of allegiance to the Sovereign and Royal Family. To swear—" I do reject and detest as impious, the belief that it is lawful to murder or destroy any person whatsoever, for, or under the pretence of their being hereticks, and also that . . . wicked principle that no faith is to be kept with hereticks . . . and I abjure the opinion that princes excommunicated by the Pope and Council, or by any authority of the See of Rome,

or by any authority whatsoever, may be deposed or murdered by their subjects. . . . I do not believe that the Pope of Rome, or any other foreign prince, prelate, state or potentate, hath or ought to have any temporal or civil jurisdiction, power, superiority or pre-eminence, directly or indirectly within this Kingdom . . . without thinking that I am or can be acquitted before God or man, or absolved of this declaration or any part thereof, although the Pope or any other person or authority whatsoever shall dispense with, or annul the same, or declare that it was null and void from the beginning." This Act goes on to declare, No person so naturalised may vote for or serve in Parliament, nor shall be entitled to hold any office unless he shall be a Protestant, and shall have resided there for three years. Excepting he hath obtained the right of voting, by such ways as others of His Majesty's subjects of this Kingdom hath hitherto, or shall hereafter obtain the same.

24 *Geo. III., c.* 56.—" Whereas divers profligate and evil disposed persons have of late with knives . . . in a barbarous . . . manner houghed, maimed and disabled several soldiers . . . by cutting the tendons and sinews of their legs across . . . and whereas the said barbarous offenders have generally escaped from justice . . . for their more speedy discovery . . . and for the support of those . . . subjects . . . as shall hereafter be houghed . . . that if such be committed . . . in any county except Dublin . . . at assizes, within one year after such fact . . . grand jury of the county shall acess the barony in £20 p. a. to be paid to such sufferer. . . . For the more effectual prevention . . . after passing of this act, every person or persons convicted of any crime or crimes in the . . . acts of 13th, 14th, 17th, 18th years of the reign of his present Majesty . . . shall be executed the day next but one after sentence passed." Regarding soldiers who were sufferers from this

horrid practice, " now in the service of our Sovereign Lord the King, by cutting the tendons and sinews of their legs across, and thereby totally disabling the said soldiers . . . from earning their bread by their labours . . . and whereas the said barbarous offenders have generally after perpetrating such enormous crimes, escaped from justice . . . for the more speedy and effectual discovery and prosecution of such offenders . . . by the advice and consent of the lords spiritual, temporal, and Commons in this Parliament assembled . . . that if . . . after the passing of the Act (any) be houghed . . . (any who) commit such offence escape . . . within one year (grand jury's) . . . charge upon the inhabitants of such barony . . . or the inhabitants of the county . . . city . . . town (except Dublin) in which the said fact shall be committed the sum of twenty pound sterling to be paid yearly, and every year during the life of . . . such subject . . . for his support and maintainence."

In Dublin, should occasion require, the Court of King's Bench in like manner levied an annual sum of £20 for such victims. Private enquiry before a set of appointed officers as to details of outrage were also ordered. If within six months the offender was found and convicted no such sum was levied. For the better prevention of "the wicked and barbarous practices mentioned and described in and by an Act of Parliament, 13 Geo. III., entitled, "*An act to prevent malicious cutting and wounding, and to punish offenders called chalkers,*" and other Acts concerning "chalkers," every person convicted of any such crimes, after the passing of this Act, *shall be executed the next day but one after sentence is passed,* unless the said day be Sunday, when execution shall be deferred until the following Monday. Prisoner to be kept apart, and fed only on bread and water. If the gaoler offend by neglecting these orders, he forfeits his employment, and is fined £50, being imprisoned until this fine be paid. This Act was ordered to be in force from June 24th, 1784, until June 24th, 1792.

25 *Geo. III., c.* 60.—Repeals the Coercion Act of 1781. In this same year a very large sum—£20,000—was levied upon the Manors of Port Dungloe and Mount Charles in the County Donegal, the estate of Lord Conyngham, to be expended, with twenty thousand other pounds granted by Parliament, in promoting the fisheries on the west coast of Donegal.

26 *Geo. III., c.* 24.—" An Act for the better execution of the law within the city of Dublin and certain parts adjacent thereto; and for quieting and protecting possessions within this kingdom, for the more expeditious transportation of felons, for reviewing, continuing and strengthening and amending certain statutes therein mentioned."

30 *Geo. III., c.* 29.—*An Act for taking away the Court of Wards and Liveries, etc.* Protestants may dispose of the tuition of their children under twenty-one to any person not professing the Popish religion. Any professing the Popish religion—*not* having lapsed from the Protestant religion— may likewise dispose of their children to any other than an ecclesiastic of the Church of Rome. Any child of a Papist taken out of the kingdom, the chancellor may make provision for the preservation of the estate until the child be brought back and delivered to a guardian.

31 *Geo. III., c.* 17.—An Act to prevent the horrid crime of murder. Repeals the Act, 10 Henry VII., concerning murder of " malice prepensed treason," and the Act of 9 Anne, for " appeal in case of murder." Orders, also, that bodies of murderers executed in Dublin to be given to the Company of Surgeons; and elsewhere to local infirmary surgeon. Bodies of murderers must be dissected or hung

in chains. Only food after conviction bread and water. Persons attempting rescue of murderers to be deemed guilty of felony, and suffer death without benefit of clergy. For attempting to rescue the body from the surgeons transportation. Persons charged with murder before this Act to be proceeded against as if this Act had not passed.

For the year 1791 horse racing was prohibited in the vicinity of Dublin, because "much idleness and drunkenness and riot have for some years past been occasioned by the frequency of horse races . . . for remedy whereof . . . it shall not be lawful for any person to cause any horse . . . to run for any public prize whatever within nine miles of his Majesty's Castle of Dublin . . . any assembly more than twelve in number . . . shall be deemed an unlawful assembly, and . . . be dispersed as such . . . persons so present prosecuted . . . proceeded against as persons present and assisting an unlawful assembly . . . horse . . . seized . . . and in eight days sold . . . money paid to the treasurer of the county." Justices may "destroy all booths, seize vessels and liquors."

31 *Geo. III.*, c. 44.—Is a revival of lapsed coercion laws.

32 *Geo. III.*, c. 21.—Act to remove Restraints . . . of subjects professing the Popish religion.

Oaths required to be taken, by recited Acts on admission to the Bar, not required to be taken by Roman Catholics after June 24th, 1792; oath of allegiance to the King to be taken instead by attorneys, solicitors, or notaries, *but those cannot be so qualified to the place or office of King's Council.* The ninth clause gives permission for Protestants to marry with Papists, but a Protestant married to a Popish wife may not vote at election. Protestant clergy may celebrate such marriages, but Dissenting ministers and Popish priests may not celebrate marriages between Protestants and

Roman Catholics. It is no longer necessary for persons professing the Popish religion to obtain licence for teaching school. Popish tradesmen at liberty to take apprentices.

32 *Geo. III.*, c. 22.—Time for Papists to take the oath and conform extended.

33 *Geo. III.*, c. 2.—" Whereas tumultuous risings have of late happened in some parts of this kingdom, and the persons engaged therein have practised various secret contrivances for being supplied with and keeping arms . . . in order to prevent . . . from 20 Feb. 1793 it shall not be lawful for any person whomsoever to import pistols, gunlocks (etc., etc.), without having first obtained a license." Penalties, heavy fines and forfeiture.

33 *Geo. III.*, c. 21 (1793).—" Whereas various Acts of Parliament have been passed, imposing on his Majesty's subjects professing the Popish or Roman Catholick religion, many restraints and disabilities, to which other subjects of this realm are not liable ; and from the peaceable and loyal demeanor of his Majesty's Popish, or Roman Catholick subjects, it is fit that such restraints and disabilities shall be discontinued. Be it therefore enacted . . . that his Majesty's subjects being Papists, or persons professing the Popish or Roman Catholick religion, or educating any of their children in that religion shall not be liable or subject to any penalties, forfeitures, disabilities or incapacities . . . touching their estates . . . real or personal, or touching the acquiring of property . . . save such as his Majesty's subjects of the Protestant religion are liable and subject to ; and that such oaths as are required to be taken by persons in order to qualify themselves for voting at elections of members to serve in Parliament . . . as import or deny that the person taking the same is a Papist, or married to a Papist . . . shall not hereafter be required to be taken by voter . . . and it shall not be necessary . . . that he should

... take the oath of allegiance or abjuration ... Provided always ... that Papists ... be hereby required to perform all qualifications ... which are now required ... in like cases ... save and except such oaths ... as are herein excepted. ...

Provided always, that nothing herein before contained shall extend ... or alter any law ... now in force, by which certain qualifications are required ... by persons enjoying any offices or places of trust under his Majesty. ... Provided ... nothing shall extend, to give Papists a right to vote at any parish vestry, for levying of money to rebuild any parish church ... or for demisal ... of the estate ... belonging to any church ... or for the salary of the parish clerk," etc. (they may keep arms if they have estates valued at £100 per annum, "*as protestants may*"). They may have and hold civil and other offices like their fellow subjects, professorships, or be fellows or masters of colleges " to be hereafter founded in this kingdom ; provided that such college shall be a member of the University of Dublin, *and shall not be founded exclusively for the education of papists* ... nor consist exclusively of masters, fellows, or other persons professing the popish religion ... and be a member of any body corporate, *except the college of the holy and undivided Trinity* of Queen Elizabeth, near Dublin ... without recieveing the sacrament of the Lord's supper, according to the rights and ceremonies of the Church of Ireland ... provided they take an oath of allegiance to the King ... that is to say—I, A. B. do hereby declare, that I do profess the Roman Catholick religion. I ... do swear that I do abjure, condemn, and detest, as unchristian and impious, the principle that it is lawful to murder, destroy, or any way injure any person whatsoever, for, or under the pretence of being an heretick ; and I do declare solemnly before God, that I believe, that no act in itself unjust, immoral or wicked, can ever be justified or excused by, or under pretence or colour, that it was done either for the good of the church, or in obedience to any ecclesiastical power whatsoever. I also do declare, that it is *not* an article of the Catholick faith, neither am I thereby required to believe or profess that the pope is infallible, *or* that I am bound to obey any order in its own nature immoral, though the pope or any ecclesiastical power should issue or direct such order, but on the contrary I hold that it would be sinful in me to pay any respect or obedience thereto." [Here follows a protestation against the power of the Pope to forgive sin.—A. M. R.] ". . . I do swear that I will defend to the utmost, the settlement and arrangement of property in this country as established by the laws now in being. I do hereby disclaim, disavow, and solemnly abjure any intention to subvert the present church establishment, for the purpose of substituting a catholick establishment in its stead; and I do solemnly swear, that I will *not* exercise any privilege to which I am, or *may* become entitled to disturb or weaken the protestant religion and protestant government in this kingdom. So help me God." Papists may be professors of medicine in Sir Patrick Dunn's. Not to sit in Parliament, be Governor of this kingdom, Lord High Chancellor, Chief Justice of the King's Bench, etc., etc., or fellow of Trinity College, *unless* he shall take the oath and perform the several requisites required by those who enjoy the said offices. They may not present to any Church benefice, neither may they perform marriages between Protestants, or Protestant and Papist under a penalty of £500. After June 1st, 1793, to admit to degrees in Trinity College by taking oath of allegiance and abjuration.

33 *Geo. III.*, *c.* 29.—To prevent election or appointment of unlawful assemblies . . . "if any person shall give or publish, or cause . . . notice of election to be holden . . .

or appointment of . . . representatives . . . shall be deemed guilty of an high misdemeanor . . . except . . . according to the charters and usages of such bodies corporate respectively. . . . Nothing herein . . . shall impede . . . his Majestys subjects . . . to petition . . . for redress of any public or private grievance."

33 *Geo. III., c.* 30. An Act to prevent, during the present War between Great Britain and France, all *traitorous correspondence* with, or aid to, His Majesty's enemies.

35 *Geo. III., c.* 21.—" Whereas, by the laws now in force in this kingdom it is not lawful to endow any College or Seminary for the education *exclusively* of persons professing the Roman Catholic religion . . . it is now become expedient that a Seminary should be established for that purpose . . . be it therefore enacted . . . that the Right Hon. John Viscount FitzGibbon, lord Chancellor of Ireland, the Right Hon. John Earl of Clonmell lord chief justice of his Majestys court of Kings bench in Ireland, the Right Hon. Hugh Lord Carleton, chief Justice of his Majesty's Court of Common pleas in Ireland, and the Right Hon. Barry Yelverton chief baron of the Court of Exchequer in Ireland, the Chancellor, or lord Keeper, chief justices and chief baron of the said Courts for the time being together with Arthur James Plunkett, commonly called Earl of Fingall, Jenico Preston, viscount Gormanstown, Sir Thomas Browne called Viscount of Kenmare, Sir Edward Bellew, Richard Strange, Sir Thomas French, Rev. Richard O'Reilly of Drogheda, D.D., Rev. John Thomas Troy, D.D., Dublin, Rev. Thomas Bray, Thurles, D.D., Rev. Boetius Egan, Tuam, D.D., Rev. Patrick Joseph Plunkett, Navan, D.D., Rev. Phillip MacDavett, Strabane, D.D., Rev. Francis Moylan, Cork, D.D., Rev. Gerald Tehan, Killarney, D.D., Rev. Daniel Delany, Tullow, D.D., Rev. Edmond French,

Athlone, D.D., Rev. Thomas Hussey, Dublin, D.D." They were empowered to receive subscriptions, acquire lands and to erect buildings, and Popish ecclesiastics were permitted to officiate in chapels appointed by said trustees for that purpose. All laws concerning the government of said academy (excepting the religious discipline thereof) to be approved by the Lord Lieutenant. Should any trustee die or resign (saving legal officials) the trustees elect a successor, who must be "a natural born subject of his Majesty." All trustees, masters, etc., to take oath of allegiance to the King, and no Protestant to be employed or taught therein. For this purpose for this year a grant of £8000 is apportioned.

36 *Geo. III.*, c. 20.—An Act to prevent tumultuous assembly; "to deter wicked and designing men from administering and taking such unlawful oaths . . . or . . . to be of any association or brotherhood . . . formed for seditious purposes, or to disturb the public peace, or to obey the orders or rules or commands of any Committee, or other body of men not lawfully constituted . . . or to assemble at the desire of any captain, leader . . . or person not having lawful authority. Or not to give evidence against any brother . . . confederate . . . or reveal . . . any illegal act . . . not being compelled by inevitable necessity . . . shall be adjudged guily of felony and suffer death without benefit of clergy . . . and any person . . . being convicted . . . of taking such oaths . . . shall be transported for life . . . inevitable necessity shall not justify . . . unless . . . within ten days after . . . if not prevented by actual force or sickness (he or she) disclose to one of his Majesty's justices of the Peace . . . all he or she knows concerning the compelling. . . ." Accessories guilty. Persons who have arms to give notice of same . . . any having arms who do not register forfeit £10, or are

imprisoned two months; for second offence forfeit £20, or are imprisoned for four months; if not registered, house searched for arms.

Clause 12 says: "and whereas in several cases instances persons who have given information against persons accused of crimes, have been murdered before trial of the person accused, in order to prevent their giving evidence ... some magistrates have been assassinated for bringing offenders to justice ... be it therefore enacted ... should any person ... give information against any person ... and before the trial of the person ... be murdered ... such evidence shall be admitted as evidence ... and ... if it shall appear ... any person giving information ... hath been murdered or maimed ... it shall be lawful ... for the Grand Jury to present ... sums ... to be paid to the personal representative of such witness." Strangers may be arrested, and committed if they do not give a satisfactory account of themselves. The Lord Lieutenant and Council may proclaim disturbed County or part of County. Inhabitants may be ordered to keep within their dwellings between Sunset and Sunrise. Men if found abroad "shall be transmitted to serve on board his Majestys navy." Justices may take the subject's arms for "Safe Keeping." This Act is full of many other details coercive of the unruly and disorderly.

36 *Geo. III.*, c. 31.—This is a most interesting Act, specially to those ladies who now take upon themselves political duties. "Whereas it is expedient that the judgement which has been required by law to be given and awarded against any woman or women in the cases of high treason, *or of petit treason* should no longer be continued, be it therefore enacted ... that from the 1st of June 1796 ... women convicted of the crime of high treason, or of petit treason, or of abetting, procuring or counselling

any petit treason shall not be that such women ... be drawn to the place of execution ... and *be burned to death,* but such ... shall be ... hanged by the neck until she ... be dead, any law or usage to the contrary thereof in anywise notwithstanding ... women ... convicted of the crime of petit treason, or aiding ... treason ... shall be subject ... to such pains and penalties as are ... declared with respect to persons convicted of wilful murder, in an Act passed 31 year of the reign of his present Majesty, entitled, *An act to prevent the horrid crime of murder and to repeal an act passed in the tenth year of King Henry the Seventh,* entitled, *An act for bringing an appeal in case of murder, notwithstanding the statute of King Henry the Seventh whereby murder is made high treason* ... women being so attainted ... shall be subject and liable to such and like forfeitures, and corruption of blood, as they severally would have been in case they had been severally attainted of the like crimes before the passing of this act."

36 *Geo. III.*, *c.* 32.—An Act to amend an Act passed in the fifteenth and sixteenth years of his Majesty's reign, entitled, An Act to prevent and punish tumultuous Risings of persons within this kingdom, and for other purposes therein mentioned.

36 *Geo. III.*, *c.* 42.—" Whereas tumultuous risings have of late happened in this kingdom ... in order to prevent the clandestine importation and secret keeping of arms ... be it enacted ... it shall not be lawful for any person whomsoever, to import ... cannon, mortars, or ordnance, guns, pistols (all sorts of arms and munition given in detail), without a licence ... it shall be lawful ... to land such arms ... for the personal defence ... upon registration and obtaining license ... (for so doing) ship ... shall be forfeited to his Majesty. ... Owners forfeit

£500, . . . master £200. . . ." Various penalties and fines for those importing, making, using or concealing arms follow in minute detail.

37 *Geo. III.*, c. 1. —" Whereas a traitorous and detestable conspiracy has been formed for subverting the existing laws and constitution; therefore, for the better preservation of his majesty, . . . for securing the peace . . . the law, the liberties of this kingdom, be it enacted . . . that every person or persons, that is, are, or shall be in prison within the Kingdom of Ireland . . . for high treason, . . . treasonable practices, or by warrant . . . by Lord Lieutenant, or chief Secretary . . . may be detained in safe custody without bail or mainprize until the first of August 1797 and the end of the next Session of parliament."

37 *Geo. III.*, c. 2.—" Whereas further exertions are now become necessary for the defence of this Kingdom, and for the preservation of the lives and properties of his Majestys subjects therein; be it enacted . . . that if any . . . loyal subjects . . . enroll themselves in troops or companies . . . during the present war, under officers having commissions from his Majesty . . . duly authorized, . . . for the protection of property, and preservation of the peace . . . every serjeant (and all so employed) shall receive . . . clothing, arms . . . pay." If any officer keeps any man on the roll who does not subscribe to the oath of loyalty to his Majesty, that officer to be fined £300."

37 *Geo. III.*, c. 10.—An Act to enable certain inhabitants of Armagh . . . injured in person or goods . . . to recover compensation by presentments. [This Act is much on the same lines as the present Act for compensation for injuries.—A. M. R.]

37 *Geo. III.*, c. 17.—Is interesting, inasmuch as it concerns the measures taken by Government for working the Wicklow Gold Mines. These mines appear to be, then as

now, more of a will-o'-the-wisp than an actual mine of wealth.

37 *Geo. III., c.* 26.—This Act deals with the then common theft by counterfeit Bank of Ireland notes, and is curious because it clearly proves how very unprotected our early bankers were.

37 *Geo. III., c.* 38.—" Recital of insurrection Act 36 Geo. III." : " Within three days after any county . . . proclaimed to be in a state of disturbance, or . . . in danger of becoming so, . . . a petty sessions shall be held . . . the justices of the peace . . . shall have power . . . to command the inhabitants to keep within doors at all unseasonable hours. . . . No prosecution, suit . . . shall be commenced, or carried on against any justice . . . or other person . . . merely on the ground that (such notices are informal).

" And to obviate doubts touching the administration or taking unlawful oaths, be it declared and enacted, that all oaths or engagements whatsoever, importing to bind the person taking . . . the same, to be of any association . . . whatsoever are unlawful oaths . . . persons . . . for administering or taking such oath . . . shall be ordered to serve in his Majestys land forces . . . or . . . to be sent as seamen."

37 *Geo. III., c.* 39.—" Whereas . . . the lives and properties of many peaceful and faithful subjects have been destroyed . . . and that . . . to suppress . . . such insurrections . . . officers and persons . . . in order to preserve public peace apprehended several . . . suspected of aiding . . . insurrections . . . promoting riot and tumults . . . of harbouring evil designs. . . . They seized arms and entered into houses . . . and done divers *acts not justifiable by law*, but which were for the public service . . . ought to be indemnified. Be it therefore enacted all personal actions . . . against the said . . . persons, for any matter

... done ... for the safety of the state ... shall be void." If any case is brought, persons sued may plead the general issue ... may claim double costs.

The next Act was to secure the punishment of those who tampered with, or endeavoured to seduce, the King's troops: they were to suffer death without benefit of clergy.

37 *Geo. III.*, c. 57.—This Act lengthened the time for persons to take the oath of allegiance, and recover their sequestered estates, as ordered by the Act of the second year of Queen Anne, to January 1st, 1798. This Act did not, however, reinstate those persons to *any office or appointment already filled up by other persons, such other persons as are now in possession to remain in possession*, as if this Act had never been made.

37 *Geo. III.*, c. 62.—" Most gracious Sovereign " . . . " Whereas . . . the Reverend Doctor William Hamilton, rector of the parish of Clondevadogue ... Raphoe ... Donegal ... was lately most cruelly massacred on account of his meritorious exertions as a magistrate," the Commons of Ireland presented Earl Camden with a petition to the King that provision be made for his widow and children. In answer to that address His Majesty " recommended " to grant " an annuity of £700 to be vested in trustees for the maintenance of the said widow ... after her decease to be divided among her children ... for their respective lives." [This sum came out of the Consolidated Fund, and was vested in Lord de Vesci and the Rev. Chamberlane Walker for the use of the Hamiltons.—A. M. R.]

The next Act was similar, requesting the King to permit allowance to be made for the widow and children of the Rev. George Knipe, rector of Castlerichard, County Meath, " lately most cruelly massacred on account of his meritorious exertions as a magistrate." Three hundred a year was given for their use, in trust to John Maxwell, Newtown

Barry, in County Wexford, Thomas Knipe, Churchill, County Meath, and John Reed, of Dublin.

38 *Geo. III.*, c. 7.—This is a Press Act, to prevent abuses arising from the publication of traitorous, seditious, false and slanderous libels. Penalties of £500 on all concerned in such publication, and press to be seized and destroyed, and those disqualified from printing or publishing henceforward. Grand juries of counties may "present" any newspaper, for such publications "as a public nuisance," and they be punished as above said.

38 *Geo. III.*, c. 10.—Deals with money matters and borrowings, to supply the needs of the country for the ensuing year. £1,500,000 borrowed from England, at £6 7s. 6d. per cent. interest; this sum being required to supplement the already impossible taxes on the country. This budget shows the following sums, which throw great light upon the amount of money spent upon "the army" required to keep the peace of the country, the "supplementing" of Irish industry, and other Government payments previous to the Union:—For Laggan Navigation, £832; for linen and hempen manufacture *in Leinster, Munster, and Connaught*, £21,600; for building churches, £5000; to Dublin Society for husbandry, £5500; for cleaning and improving Dublin streets, £10,000; for hospitals and schools, £44,140 (£10,302 5s. 10d. of this was for Catholick College of Maynooth, "for the better educating of persons professing the Popish or Roman Catholick religion, to enable them to complete the building of the Catholic Seminary of Maynooth and for other purposes"); for the Civil Service, £102,624 was required; of this £2500 went to apprehending criminals, £25,000 to Solicitor employed in criminal cases; for the army of land force in Ireland, £3,400,596 was needed; on *French* ministers (conformist) at St. Patrick's, £150; at Cork, £100;

Lisburn, Dundalk, and Innoshannon, £60 each; Waterford and Portarlington, £50 each; while, in Dublin, a German minister was paid £50; the prison chaplain received £20; the Rector of St. Paul's for attending the military, £52 18s. 2d.; the Chaplain of Marchelsea also £52 18s. 2d.; while the chaplain to garrison at Charlemont was paid £42 6s. 7d.

38 *Geo. III.*, c. 14.—Continues the Coercion Act of last year.

38 *Geo. III.*, c. 16.—Renews the Arms and Alien Act.

38 *Geo. III.*, c. 17.—Voluntary Contributions Act, for the defence of the country.

38 *Geo. III.*, c. 19.—Another Act for protection of those engaged in putting down sedition.

38 *Geo. III.*, c. 21.—Reinforces and strengthens previous Acts for the suppression of insurrection. Places for trying same may be changed. All found with arms required to give them up, and to be deemed disorderly, and dealt with accordingly. Any persons making or selling arms or pikes without Government licence to be transported for seven years.

38 *Geo. III.*, c. 25.—An Act for the better execution of the law and preservation of the public peace.

38 *Geo. III.*, c. 37.—If foreign troops are needed to be brought in for defence of the country, they are to be treated in a similar manner as His Majesty's regular army.

38 *Geo. III.*, c. 46.—English militia offer, to come over and help to quell the insurrection, accepted. Regular or militia officers of Ireland shall not sit in Court Martial on British Militia, or *vice versâ*.

38 *Geo. III.*, c. 50.—Act for better collection of sums— fines, gaol deliveries, etc., of persons confined for "treasonable practices."

38 *Geo. III.*, c. 55.—An Act for the King's most gracious and free pardon. The King . . . being desirous to show his royal inclination to mercy . . . considering that divers

... have rendered themselves obnoxious to the laws, and subject to the highest penalties, by . . . unnatural rebellion . . . from which they can in nowise be freed, but by his Majesty's goodness . . .; and that some of his Majesty's subjects in suppressing . . . the said rebellion, may have done divers acts, which could not be justified by the strict terms of law . . . hath resolved . . . to grant his general and free pardon . . . not doubting, but that however it may be received by those who are obstinately bent on the ruin of their country, it will raise a due sense of gratitude in all who have been artfully misled into treasonable practices . . . and preserve 'them and others, from standing in need of the like mercy for the future, when such clemency may not be so expedient for the public welfare, as it would be agreeable to his Majesty's inclination: and hoping that all his subjects, by this act of grace will be induced henceforth with more cheerfulness and affection to apply themselves in discharge of their respective duties to his Majesty, and to live in a loyal and dutiful obedience to him. Therefore . . . all and every his Majesty's subjects . . . of Ireland, their heirs, successors, executors, and administrators . . . shall be acquitted, pardoned, released, and discharged . . . of and from such treasons, misprisions of treasons, felonies, seditions, and unlawful meetings, treasonable and seditious words or libels . . . riots, routs, offences, contempts, trespasses, pains of death, pains corporal and pains pecuniary, and generally of and from all such other things, causes, quarrels, suits . . . made, done, committed . . . in prosecuting . . . said rebellion, or in suppressing . . . the same, before or until August 22nd, 1798. . . . " His Majesty grants to all subjects all goods forfeited by such treason *not hereafter excepted.*" Those excepted—"all persons being in actual custody January 1st, 1795 . . . all manner of deliberate murders, petty treasons and wilful poisonings, as also, all and all manner of conspiracies to murder . . . done committed or entered into respectively, and all and every accessories of the same offences . . . also excepted . . . persons who have been enrolled or commissioned in troops or companies . . . persons conspiring . . . for invading . . . or procuring invasion of this realm . . . also . . . members of any committees . . . known by the name . . . of Executive or National committees . . . of united Irishmen . . . also . . . all . . . who acted as generals, majors or captains . . . in any army . . . levied for the prosecution of the said most horrid and unnatural rebellion . . . Also . . . persons . . . who shall not deliver up arms, or . . . such . . . as shall be attainted of high treason . . . or court martial since 24 May 1798, in . . . being concerned in the said unnatural rebellion. Also . . . all excepted out of this pardon, all offences committed or done, since 1st Nov. 1797 against any Act for the punishment of mutiny and desertion." And also except (here follow a list of thirty-one names of persons specially named, three of them being clergy—one, the Rev. Arthur M'Mahon, Holywood, County Down, priest; the others, Rev. James Townsend, Grey Abbey, County Down, and the Rev. James Hull, formerly near Bangor, in the same county). His Majesty reserves judgment, and may extend mercy on such conditions as he shall think fit to persons excepted.

38 *Geo. III.*, cc. 58-60.—Loan of £1,500,000 from England. Respectively deal with details of confusions caused by the rebellion, c. 60, being to legalise actions of corporations which, owing to rebellion, were unable to assemble on the days appointed by their charters. The officers to be deemed officers until new elections are made. This Act touches Elections of Provost and Fellows of Trinity College.

38 *Geo. III., c.* 68.—A commission appointed to enquire into losses, of sufferings in loyal subjects, during the subsisting rebellion in this kingdom.

38 *Geo. III., c.* 72.—An Act for Sale of His Majesty's Quit Rents, Crown and other Rents, *and of lands forfeited in 1641 and 1688, and other lands remaining undisposed of.* This is a lengthy Act, full of details, and enacts that those in possession of lands as "collectors" of the King's rent, have *just right* to purchase, *but not under sixteen years' purchase.* If they pay one-tenth of purchase money within six months, the remainder may be paid in three quarterly payments. In default of payment on one quarter day, so much as was paid to be forfeited. After six months no preference given to "collectors," or occupiers, but land to be sold to the highest bidder *not under sixteen years' purchase,* to be paid for as before mentioned. "The Bank of Ireland may advance a million on credit of said rents at 5 per cent." *for the immediate use of His Majesty's Government.*

38 *Geo. III., c.* 74.—Another Act for indemnifying persons who suffered for the preservation of the public peace by suppressing the insurrection.

38 *Geo. III., c.* 78.—Is an Act to prevent those transported, etc., on account of the present rebellion, from going to countries at war with His Majesty. Having expressed their contrition, they are pardoned, but may not at present return to this country. A list is here given of those who are in custody for high treason, and confess themselves guilty of the same. Amongst them are two Popish priests —one being the Rev. James Bushe, the other, Rev. John Barrett, both of Dublin—and Thomas Addis Emmett. If any of these men return without permission, they are to be transported for life.

38 *Geo. III., c.* 80.—An Act to compel persons who have been engaged in rebellion to surrender within a

limited time, or else they be attainted of high treason. A list of names of those attainted is here given. Amongst these is Napper Tandy and Wolfe Tone. They are all to be "attainted of High Treason, unless they surrender themselves . . . on or before 1 Dec. 1798.

38 *Geo. III.*, *c.* 82.—Is an Act to license all who hold arms: without licence no one to hold arms.

40 *Geo. III.*, *c.* 18.—Persons in prison for treasonable practices to be detained in safe custody, without bail or mainprize, until March 25th, 1801. Plans of safe keeping may be changed by warrants.

40 *Geo. III.*, *c.* 19.—" Whereas an Act passed in England in the eighth year of Rich. 2, entitled, "No man of law shall be justice of assize or gaol delivery in his own county," which Act is now of force in this kingdom by the Statute law thereof . . . and it is expedient that such part of the said law shall not be of force in this kingdom, . . . be it enacted . . . that so much of the Said Act shall not be of force in this kingdom.

40 *Geo. III.*, *c.* 23.—" Whereas by several Acts of Parliament in force in this kingdom . . . the burning of land by any tenant without the permission of his landlord has been declared to be an offence . . . prohibited under a penalty which is not sufficient to prevent the evil practice . . . after the 25 March 1800 any person . . . burn the Soil or surface of the earth, or cause or permit the soil . . . to be burned, shall . . . forfeit the sum of ten pounds (exclusive of the rent payable by such person) for every Irish acre so to be burned.

40 *Geo. III.*, *c.* 29.—" An Act to regulate the mode by which Lords Spiritual and temporal and the Commons to serve in the United Kingdom on the Part of Ireland, shall be summoned and returned to the said Parliament."

Thursday, the 12 June 1800, Royal Assent given.

"Whereas it is agreed by the 4th article of Union 4 lords Spiritual, 28 lords temporal and 100 commoners are to sit and vote on the part of Ireland. Two for each County of Ireland, two for the city of Dublin, two for the city of Cork, one for the College of the Holy Trinity of Dublin, and one each for the 31 most considerable cities, towns and boroughs. Spiritual peers, one Archbishop and three bishops in each Session by rotation. Armagh, Dublin, Cashel and Tuam," and so by rotation of sessions for ever. Meath, Kildare, Derry, were the three bishops for the first Session and so on they are all named to follow in rotation, the lord bishop of Clonfert and Kilmacduagh being the last named, "the said rotation to be . . . subject to such variation as hereinafter provided. The 28 temporal lords to be chosen by all the temporal peers of Ireland, to sit until death or forfeiture. Any person summoning for an election save in the 32 counties and 36 named boroughs shall be punished according to the Act 16 Rich. 2. On the day following royal assent for the Union, the Primate, the bishops of Meath, Kildare and Derry shall be the representatives for first Session. On the Same day at 12 oc. lords temporal shall meet and elect 28 peers. That is to say the names of the Peers shall be called over by the clerk of the crown or deputy, and each peer . . . who has actually Sat in the house of Lords of Ireland, and who . . . have taken the oaths . . . by law required, shall deliever himself, or by proxy, a list of twenty eight temporal peers . . . to the clerk, who shall then and there publickly read the lists . . . and declare the 28 chosen by the majority of votes." If a spiritul peer, being also a temporal peer, is chosen as a temporal peer, he sits as such, and drops out of the rotation of bishops. The present members of the Parliament of Great Britain and the members of the present Irish Parliament for the counties shall form the first United Parliament.

With regard to Trinity College, and the boroughs and cities (having two members), they, or any five of them, shall meet the Clerk of the Crown in the House of Commons. Their names shall all be written on separate pieces of paper, folded, and placed in a glass or glasses, and the first drawn name of members sitting for each of those places shall be the member to serve for the said place in the first Parliament of the United Kingdom. If one member withdraw his name for one of these seats, the other be the member. If both withdraw, and if the writ be issued for election in their place, two shall be chosen accordingly, and then they shall be drawn by lot. Other vacancies shall be filled hereafter by resolution of the United Parliament.

40 *Geo. III.*, c. 34.—By this Act, Lord Lieutenant may apoint five Commissioners to ascertain what allowances should be paid to bodies corporate or individuals, in respect to those cities, towns, and boroughs, which shall cease to return any member to serve in Parliament, from and after the Union. Each Commissioner to have £1200 per annum, and expenses. The sum to be paid for each disfranchised place not to exceed £15,000. For the offices done away with by the Union, those who now enjoy them shall have salary for their lives, if on civil list; if otherwise, allowances to be made: the sum of £1,400,000 granted for this purpose. Sums awarded to be paid as follows: by five half-yearly intalments of twenty *per centum* each on the principal sums, with interest of 5 per cent., from January 1st, 1801, until all be paid.

40 *Geo. III.*, c. 38.—"An Act for the Union of Great Britain and Ireland." "*Article first*: ... from 1st January 1801 the said Kingdoms shall 'for ever be united into one Kingdom.' *Article second*: that the Succession of the Crown continue as at present. *Article third*: one parliament. *Article fourth*: (as to the representation as

before arranged) Irish peers, who are not representative, may sit as British Commoners. The first united parliament, so constituted, shall sit so long as the present parliament of Great Britain may now by law continue to sit, if not sooner dissolved. 'Provided always that until an Act shall have passed in the United Kingdom, providing in what case persons holding offices or places of profit under the Crown in Ireland, shall be incapable of being members of the House of Commons, of the Parliament of the United Kingdom . . . the lords of Parliament on the part of Ireland, in the House of Lords of the United Kingdom, shall at all times have the same privileges of parliament, which shall belong to the lords of parliament on the part of Great Britain, and the lords spiritual and temporal respectively on the part of Ireland . . . the same rights . . . as peers of Great Britain, the spiritual lords of Ireland of the same rank and degree of Great Britain, shall have rank and precedency next, and immediately after the lords spiritual of the same rank and degree of Great Britain, . . . and shall enjoy all privileges as fully as the lords spiritual of Great Britain do now or may hereafter enjoy the same . . . the right of sitting on the trial of peers excepted. *Article five*: 'The churches of England and Ireland, as now by law established, be united into one Protestant episcopal church, to be called "the United church of England and Ireland," the doctrine, worship, discipline and government . . . shall remain in full force forever, as the same are now by law established in the church of England; and that the continuance and preservation of the said United Church, as the Established church of England and Ireland, shall be deemed and taken to be the essential and fundamental part of the Union . . . and be preserved as the same are now established by law and by the acts for the Union of the two Kingdoms of

England and Scotland.' *Article sixth*: 'Subjects of Great Britain and Ireland to be on the same footing from 1st January 1801, as to encouragement of growth, produce or manufactures, trade and navigation. No duty on produce of one country to the other. Excepted articles in schedule to pay duty for 20 years.' *Article seven*: 'Charges for debts of either kingdom before Union shall be separately defrayed. For 20 years after the Union the proportion of expenditure of the United Kingdoms be as 15 to 2. If the Irish revenue in any year exceed the interest on debt, sinking fund and proportionall contribution, taxes to that amount shall be reduced, or the surplus applied by the united parliament to local Irish purposes. All monies raised after the Union shall be a joint debt. Parliament may declare exemptions of special taxes in Scotland and Ireland. Premiums for agricultural, manufactures and pious purposes shall be given by the united parliament to Ireland for twenty years, in the same proportions as have been voted by the Irish parliament for the last six years. *Article eight*: All laws in force at time of the Union, in civil and ecclesiastical Courts, within the respective kingdoms, *shall remain* as now by law established, subject to alterations from time to time as circumstances may appear to the United Parliament to require." Tenth clause of this article permits the King to continue "the Privy Council of Ireland," for that part of the United Kingdom called Ireland, "so long as he shall think fit."

40 *Geo. III.*, c. 44.—"Whereas it is necessary more effectually to prevent persons from returning to his Majesty's dominions, who have been, or shall be transported, banished; or who, to avoid prosecution have absented themselves on account of Rebellion, any found at large after 1st August 1800, without license shall be adjudged a felon, and shall on conviction, for the first

offence, recieve such corporal punishment as the Court shall award, and be transported for his or her natural life. If such persons again return they shall suffer death as a felon without benefit of clergy."

40 *Geo. III.*, c. 49.—" Whereas 38 & 39 Geo. III. have not dealt with all the 'loyal sufferers' during the late rebellion, and . . . there are many poor and pitiable claimants, time to claim extended to three months after passing of this act. 'In consequence of the rebellious atrocities so generally perpetrated through a considerable part of the County Galway, by the horrid practise of houghing, maiming and mutilating sheep and black cattle, burning houses, barns, ricks, losses in such case to be compensated at the rate of 95 *per cent.* where the sum certified exceeds £100; £90 where it exceeds £200 and so until £500. If £500 and not £1000 at 75 p.c. From one to three thousand at £70 p.c. Three to five thousand £60 p.c., etc., etc. This Act also secured compensation to loyal landlords who have suffered by disloyal tenants. Two grants of £1500 were made to enable the King to provide for widows and orphans of those who suffered in the rebellion, and also to reward those 'instrumental in the preservation of the loyal inhabitants from massacre,' or by the discovery of traitors."

40 *Geo. III.*, c. 50.—" Whereas, after the Union the duties of several officers . . . of the two houses of parliament of Ireland will cease . . . it is . . . just compensation be made to such persons . . . for the loss of emolument . . . There shall be paid . . . in manner as herinafter mentioned . . . annuities and compensation severally for their respective losses. In accordance with published Schedule the House of Lords, beginning with the speaker, Lord Clare, who recieved £3978 3s. 4d., and ending with Andrew Bowen the water porter, allotted £4 11s., over £13,000

was divided amongst those of the House of Lords, including clerks, ushers, doorkeepers, housekeeper and housemaids. In the Commons the same proceeding was adopted. The Hon. John Foster, speaker, recieved £5085 8s. 4d., and so on all down to Mary Connor, house attendant £4 11s., each one who personally suffered by 'the loss of office at the Union' received compensation."

APPENDIX.

GRATTAN'S VIEW OF IRISH PARLIAMENT.

1779. Grattan, when debating the address upon the opening of Parliament, said :—"The distresses of this kingdom are twofold—the beggary of the people, and the bankruptcy of the State." . . . He asked indignantly—"Whether there were not too many people in the kingdom?" [There were then about three millions.—A. M. R.] "Was there one rich merchant in the Kingdom?" (This Parliament had to borrow £1,660,000 from England at 6 per cent. to keep the country going.—A. M. R.]

1790-1. After Grattan had obtained his Free Parliament, he asked—"What has our renewed Constitution produced? . . . Any great or good measure? No. A Police Bill—a Press Bill—a Riot Act—a great increase of pensions—fourteen new places for members of Parliament, and a most notorious and corrupt sale of peerages. Where will it end?"

[Between 1791 and 1800 expenditure of Irish Government increased year by year from $7\frac{1}{2}$ millions to 17 millions per annum, while export and import duties were reduced £1,500,000 per annum.—A. M. R.]

1790-1. "The projected administration . . . will make the Minister completely absolute. It will procure a legislature ready to allow any measure according as the Divan of the Castle . . . give word of command. . . . That Court will be free from control ; its first idea will be plunder. . . . Past administrations have proved such a Court . . . a political high life below stairs. . . . This Court would soon lose the esteem of all moderate and rational individuals. Already such men are disgusted. . . . they can't approve of what they know your only principle of Government, the omnipotence of corruption. . . . Do you imagine that the laws of this country can retain due authority under a system such as yours . . . a system which not only poisons the source of laws, but pollutes the seat of judgment? You may say that justice between man and man will be faithfully administered ; . . . the laws in a free country will not retain their authority unless the people are protected by them against plunder and oppression ; . . . the friends of that Administration may talk plausibly on the subject of public tranquillity ; . . . *they are the ringleaders of sedition placed in authority.* . . . Supposing the country willing to give up her liberty, and willing to give away her money, yet will she surrender her money merely for the purpose of enabling such a set of Ministers to take away her liberty?"

[These are Grattan's descriptive words of his own time. How different from Mr. Gladstone's fancy sketch of the peace and prosperity of that time!—A. M. R.]

Though this pamphlet has been delayed in publication, I have not had an opportunity of thoroughly revising my notes.— A. M. R.

May 10*th*, 1893.

www.ingramcontent.com/pod-product-compliance
Lightning Source LLC
Chambersburg PA
CBHW020100170426
43199CB00009B/354